THE CINEMA OF
ANDRZEJ WAJDA

Wajda is undoubtedly the greatest
Polish film director, and this definitive
monograph by his country's most
prominent film critic analyses the appeal and significance of such masterpieces as *A Generation*, *Ashes and
Diamonds*, and *Everything for Sale*.

$2.95/£1.10

The Cinema of
Andrzej WAJDA

by Bolesław Michałek

Translated by EDWARD ROTHERT

London: The Tantivy Press
South Brunswick and New York: A. S. Barnes and Company

BOLESŁAW MICHAŁEK, born 1925, a graduate of the École des Sciences Politiques et Sociales at Brussels University.
Film critic, long-time editor of the Warsaw weekly "Film," and author of numerous books on the cinema—"The Art of Facts" ("Sztuka faktów"), "Essays on Polish Cinema" ("Szkice o filmie polskim"), "Dreams and Reality" ("Marzenia i rzeczywistość"), "The Cinema of Our Day" ("Kino naszych czasów").
For many years chairman of the Film Critics' Club in Warsaw, and one-time chairman of FIPRESCI (International Federation of the Film Press).

The Publishers wish to thank the Author and Film Polski for the illustrations used in this book.

© Copyright 1973 by The Tantivy Press
and Bolesław Michałek

English translation, first published 1973,
© copyright by The Tantivy Press

Cover design by Stefan Dreja

LC No: 72-9939
SBN 0 498 01325 1 (U.S.A.)
SBN 9007 3067 6 (U.K.)

Printed in the United States of America

Contents

PN
1998
A3
W244

Wajda during the filming of SIBERIAN LADY MACBETH

Introduction

THERE ARE in the history of the cinema directors whose films are self-explanatory: they explore universal themes within a readily recognisable frame of reference. But there are others whose *oeuvre,* like an iceberg, is only partly exposed to view, and effort, knowledge and imagination are required to visualise its real dimensions and features. Are the former the only works worthy of attention, and the latter merely of relative value? One such phenomenon which cannot be understood without a map is the cinema of Andrzej Wajda, for the excellent reason that its main and continually recurring current springs from the complex, dramatic and little-known history of Poland—especially its most recent period, the conflict-racked years of the last war. What is more, history is not merely a backcloth to the drama in his films, but their central concern.

There is nothing of the successful cosmopolitan film-maker about Wajda. He was born and has always lived in Poland, and is very much a creature of her history, her mythology and her art (both high and low). In all his films he keeps bandying the concepts, the common coinage, the fantasies of the Polish literary and philosophical tradition which always strike a chord in his own country but have none too clear a ring outside its borders. Finally, his own personal tastes and idiosyncrasies, his loves and his hates, his unique type of sensibility, give him a penchant for overstatement, for spectacular effects and symbols. One of the labels with which he has been marked is "baroque," but his symbols are not drawn from any of the stock Twentieth century canons such as Freud. "I would," he has said, "gladly trade in this clutch of national symbols—sabres, white horses, red poppies, rowanberries—for a handful of sexual symbols from the Freudian textbook. The trouble is that I just wasn't brought up on Freud. My situation is hopeless—I caught on too late." His symbolism is, therefore, parochial, rooted in the soil from which he sprang, the environment in which he grew up, and the age by which he was moulded.

This is probably why Wajda's films have never echoed as loudly as they deserve; moreover, their historical, social, and even political implications have often enough proved baffling. Western critics have detected in his art "despair" and "baroque elements," "bitterness" and "love of life"; what would be more to the point would be to dig down to the particular moods, hopes and anxieties of the country with which he is so closely involved, since, contrary to appearances, his films have never been a reflection of private crises of despair or doubt. All along, they have kept track of contemporary changes, of the psychological, social and political evolution of Poland from 1954 to the present day.

In the early Sixties, when his major films reached France, there were those who found them "controversial" on aesthetic grounds. In "Cahiers du Cinéma," for instance, there appeared an article under the pointed title "Strip-tease polonais" which referred to "the nihilism of a provincial aesthete."[1] In fact, if Wajda's art *is* controversial, it is principally in the area of content—historical, social, and political. No further proof is needed than the endless, heated, and occasionally acrimonious wrangles in Poland over the messages of each of his films. Some of them have even detonated resounding socio-political debates which have ranged far beyond the cinema and art. Here lies the chief source of their immense vitality.

Wajda, with Zygmunt Malanowicz at left, during filming of the party sequence in HUNTING FLIES

1. 'I Was Brought Up in a Barracks'

"I WAS BROUGHT UP in a cavalry barracks. I can remember watching gun carriages drawn by three pairs of horses come hurtling in at a gallop. These weren't the sort of cavalrymen you see in London at the Changing of the Guard. It was a real cavalry trained to fight wars and kill the enemy. For me they were living people whom I saw, liked, and knew; not puppets."[1]

This reminiscence speaks volumes. Wajda was born on March 6, 1927, in Suwałki, north-east Poland, one of those small towns in which the army barracks forms one of the main features of the landscape. His father was a professional officer, his mother a schoolteacher. Subsequently, like most service families, the Wajdas moved from post to post, almost always in the provinces. Such a childhood was bound to leave an imprint on Wajda's mentality, and in an interview with Bolesław Sulik he has said: "I am one of the few people who has seen artillery practice, sabre cuts and lance thrusts, *dressage*, a whole infantry regiment returning to camp on skis, funerals where the coffins were mounted on *caissons*—all visual experiences which have no doubt surfaced in my films. And they're experiences which I don't think have yet been fully tapped; some day perhaps I'll succeed in making a film about one of these remote, provincial army posts, told in the spirit of Chekhov maybe, of Russian rather than of Polish literature, since I can't see any equivalent of that desolate provincial life in Polish literature."[2] It is worth remembering that the army in those years was something more than a military organisation: it was a torch-bearer of ancient tradition, the most conspicuous emblem of the independence recently recovered after 150 years of servitude, an object of pride, with its own ethic and its own legend.

When the war broke out Wajda was only thirteen, and eighteen when it ended. However, all that he has depicted on the screen and which forms the nucleus of his work—the cavalry charges of 1939, the Warsaw resistance during the occupation, the Warsaw Rising in 1944, the liberation in 1945—are not a record of his own direct experience. During the occupation, he has said, "I only just took part in the underground and my experience was very modest";[3] and elsewhere: "I was, it is true, a soldier in the Home Army, but I had a posting of no significance and the German reprisals never came near me. . . . So I imagine that my war films, especially the first three, or even four, because I'd include *Lotna* in this category, are a kind of compensation for the stirring and exciting lives that others led, whereas I had the good fortune to escape these grim and shattering experiences."[4]

Wajda spent the occupation years in the provinces and worked at a variety of odd jobs, in one of them assisting in the restoration of paintings in a church in Radom. When peace came in 1945, he completed his secondary schooling and entered the Fine Arts Academy in Kraków where for the next three years he mingled with the city's young artists. One of these was Andrzej Wróblewski, a painter whose work has come to be recognised as one of the most original developments in post-war Polish art. Its use of a surrealistic idiom to express the harrowing tragedy of the times through which Poland had just passed give it a certain affinity with Wajda's films, especially evident in *Lotna*. Twenty years later when "Andrzej," the film director in *Everything for Sale,* visits an art gallery in the hope of recovering his bearings, the exhibition chosen is one of paintings by Wróblewski.

In 1949 Wajda left the Academy without graduating, but with a visual instinct and a fondness for a certain type of imagery that were fully formed. He transferred to the newly-opened Film School in Łódź. Was it because he felt he could express himself better in the cinema than in painting? His usual answer is that he was "looking for an open-air job."

He studied in Łódź from 1950 to 1952, retaining at the same time his interests in painting—together with a fellow-student, Konrad Nałęcki, he wrote an absorbing study of composition in the films of Eisenstein which was published in the quarterly "Kwartalnik filmowy." He also made a number of shorts as part of the School course. The first of these, *While You Sleep (Kiedy ty śpisz)*, was based on some poems by Tadeusz Kubiak devoted to the people who work at night "while you sleep." It was an attempt to marry verse to reportage and music, along the lines of the British documentaries of the Thirties—but one that was not really successful. Somewhat undistinguished as such exercises go, it came as a disappointment to Wajda. His second effort, *The Bad Boy (Zły chłopiec)*, an adaptation of a Chekhov story, was no more satisfying: designed as an echo of Nineteenth-century painting, the film was let down by its mis-handled literary content. A more rewarding experience was his third-year film, *The Pottery of Iłża (Ceramika iłżecka)*, which not only captured the beauties latent in the rough, gnarled forms of folk art, but also tried to probe deeper and bring out the counterpoint between the passing of craftsmen's generations and the durability of their artifacts.

Above: the director Andrzej (Andrzej Lapicki) at the art gallery in EVERYTHING FOR SALE. Below: Wajda (right) playing cavalryman with his brother

Wajda's qualifying work was his script contribution to a portmanteau picture, *Three Stories* (*Trzy opowieści*), inspired by the most enterprising and probably the most popular teacher at the Film School, Antoni Bohdziewicz. Made by a number of graduates of the director's and cameraman's department, it gained a general release but aroused only mild interest. Pitched in an uplifting, sermonising key, the "three stories" were about young people entering adult life. Wajda was the co-author of the screenplay along with the project's sponsor, Professor Bohdziewicz, and a young writer, Bohdan Czeszko.

About this time, at the turn of 1953, Aleksander Ford, then a key figure in Polish cinema, was planning a more serious film about youth, *Five Boys from Barska Street* (*Piątka z ulicy Barskiej*), and judged Wajda promising enough to be taken on as his assistant. This collaboration with Ford was Wajda's first major formative experience—coming in 1954, a year when far-reaching changes in both the Polish cinema and elsewhere were in the air.

2.   The Contours of the Polish Cinema *circa* 1954

IN 1954 annual production was still in single figures and the total number of features some way short of the hundred mark. But the excitement surrounding the cinema was incomparably greater, and it had come to occupy a fairly prominent place in the hierarchy of the arts.

The beginnings were immediately after the war, when the handful of film-makers still left alive started to work, without studio facilities or equipment, in a converted gymnasium in Łódź. In 1947 there appeared the first post-war film, *Forbidden Songs* (*Zakazane piosenki*), made by a popular pre-war director, Leonard Buczkowski. A sentimental, bitter-sweet evocation of events, moods and ballads from the occupation years, it proved highly successful, the day of opening having much of the atmosphere of a national holiday. What it had succeeded in doing was to strike a note that perfectly matched the temper of the times. In that same year, 1947, Eugeniusz Cękalski, one of the pre-war *Avant-garde* who had spent the war years abroad, made *Bright Fields* (*Jasne łany*), a social homily about the agrarian reform. Naive and bungled, it was an unqualified failure—though hardly the national disaster suggested by the uproar that followed: a flood of angry articles, protests, and letters to the press, not to mention thousands of jokes which filled the humorous magazines. The only reason for mentioning this storm in a teacup is that the tendency for public opinion to over-react to the products of the Polish industry remains as much a feature of the film scene now as it was twenty-five years ago.

Eventually more accomplished examples of film-making came along. There was Wanda Jakubowska's stark picture of the "concentration world" of Auschwitz, *The Last Stage* (*Ostatni etap*); the first post-war film from Aleksander Ford (a veteran director of the Left), *Border Street* (*Ulica Graniczna*), a story of Jewish children caught up in the horrors of the ghetto and its destruction; and Leonard Buczkowski's appealing comedy *The Treasure* (*Skarb*), which showed with typical "Warsaw humour" the ruined city struggling back to normality.

Although these early years produced no masterpieces, it was clear that a radical change had come over film-making in comparison with pre-war days. Gone were the conventions of the international commercial cinema and its backwater in the Poland of the Thirties; in their place was an unmistakable commitment to historical and social relevance. Each of the new films, even the hapless *Bright Fields,* tried to mesh individual experience with the mechanism of the community's destinies and, in doing so, carved out a new place for the cinema. In contrast to pre-war days, when it had existed in a form of limbo, the product of a sub-culture, wholly adrift from the other arts, the cinema now began to mine the richer seams of the literary and artistic tradition of the country—so much so that there came a time when it became the richest area of Polish artistic life.

Before then, however, about 1950, there materialised (and not only in the cinema) certain complications, with an over-rigorous version of "socialist realism." This amounted, essentially, to a set of rules which prescribed exactly the kind of person the "positive" and the "negative hero" should be, the way he ought to be "typical," or representative of his segment of society, the limits to which personal and group conflicts could be taken, and the people who could and the people who must appear in supporting roles—all in all, a codified picture of the world which was seen, hopefully, as a paean of praise to the country's social and political fabric. The result was a string of films that were dismally vapid and formula-bound. Almost all of them professed to be contemporary pictures, but bore less resemblance to the

13

actual lines of society in the early Fifties than to an idealised dream of life as it should be. Inept, disingenuous and transfixingly dull, they went some way to cooling the enthusiasm the cinema had commanded after the war. As it happened, this period was relatively short-lived in Poland, and in any case, against all odds, certain films were made which succeeded in rising above the limitations and taboos of the accepted orthodoxy. One example was Jerzy Kawalerowicz's mature *A Night to Remember/Under the Phrygian Star* (*Celuloza*).

Another, if so qualified, was *Five Boys from Barska Street* made by Aleksander Ford in 1954—with Wajda working as his assistant. By that time the aesthetic canon was being challenged, and this process shows quite distinctly in the film. Ford's idea was to show a band of delinquent youths (hooligans, thieves, even saboteurs) being straightened out by the edifying influence of honest work. This in itself was a breach of the rules which emphatically drew the line at any hint of villainy in the principal characters, even if they were due to turn over a new leaf. Secondly, in the screenplay the hero was killed at the end of the film; but this was going too far. In the final scene of the finished film he is fatally wounded, while an off-screen voice intones: "He must live!"—a reassurance that the doctrine was intact and the hero not lost. The interest of this film, however, is not confined to such signs of the times, and *Five Boys* was in fact one of the better films of the Fifties, made with considerable authority and free of the grosser oversimplifications that were then commonplace. The reason for dwelling on its incongruities is that they are revealing of the cross-currents of the period.

It was also a time when a reorganisation of the industry was impending. In 1950 production had in effect been taken over by a government department. In 1955 this system was scrapped and replaced by a new one, modelled on a blueprint prepared earlier by the film world. The centre of gravity was shifted to production groups called "Film-Makers' Units" ("Zespoły Realizatorów Filmowych") comprising directors, screenwriters, cameramen, etc. and run on a self-managing basis. Each of these units was headed by a well-known director (e.g. "Studio" by Aleksander Ford, "Start" by Wanda Jakubowska, "Kadr" by Jerzy Kawalerowicz) assisted by a *dramaturg,* invariably a writer with screen credits (e.g. Tadeusz Konwicki, Aleksander Ścibor-Rylski, Jerzy Stefan Stawiński). The groups had wide powers: control over choice of subject and script (which, however, required the approval of the ministry providing the finance), casting, renting of studios, production schedules, etc. Thus, although any money made or lost was a matter for the exchequer, the film-makers' freedom of decision and range of responsibility were appreciable. Apart from a few modifications, this system is still in force.

Meanwhile, the first graduates of the Łódź Film School had been appearing on the scene. Wajda was one of them; so were Andrzej Munk, Kazimierz Kutz, Janusz Nasfeter, Janusz Morgenstern, Tadeusz Chmielewski and cameramen like Jerzy Lipman and Jerzy Wójcik. The impact of this combination of circumstances—the reform of the industry and the infusion of new blood—was explosive and almost instantaneous. Without so much as a penny's worth of investment in new sound stages, laboratories, cameras, lighting equipment, etc., production rose from five films a year to ten, twenty and eventually twenty-five. It was a doubly-fortunate occurrence: not only had the new organisation happily coincided with the arrival of a new generation, but it should also be remembered that the context in which this happened was the intellectual and political ferment which had been brewing since 1954–5 and which came to a head with the events of October 1956.

In the first flush of these changes it seemed that the cinema would be carried away by the popular mood into crusading social criticism. From Andrzej Munk there came in 1957 *Man on the Track* (*Człowiek na torze*), written by Jerzy S. Stawiński, an indictment of the stifling atmosphere of recent years; from Jerzy Zarzycki *Land* (*Ziemia*), about the plight of a country man confronted by collectivisation; from a group of students at the Łódź Film School, under the guidance of the indefatigable Antoni Bohdziewicz, *End of the Night* (*Koniec nocy*), a trenchant look at the youth problem; and Jerzy Zarzycki followed up *Land* with *Lost Affections* (*Zagubione uczucia*), an impassioned protest at the predicament of the working woman. The quality of these films was uneven: some were heavy-handed, some meretricious. All, however, were guided by the same bearings, and a pattern to film-making seemed to take shape. So it was that the significance of a film with the pointed title of *A Generation* passed unnoticed. Only later did it transpire that it had foreshadowed what was to be the most important and richest vein in Polish cinema.

Tadeusz Łomnicki as Stach in A GENERATION

3. *A Generation* and a Generation

AFTER WORKING as Aleksander Ford's assistant on *Five Boys,* Wajda began lining up a project of his own. The fact that Ford, at the time the most influential figure in the film world, agreed to act as "artistic supervisor" dispelled any misgivings, and in 1954 *A Generation (Pokolenie)* went on the floor.

What was the "generation" of the title? "Immediately after the war," Wajda has said, "there were three films which played a certain role and gave us a lot to talk about: Aleksander Ford's *Border Street (Ulica Graniczna)*, Wanda Jakubowska's *The Last Stage (Ostatni etap)* and Jerzy Zarzycki's *Unvanquished City (Miasto niepokonane)*. These three films set out to show us our past; but the judgement pronounced by that generation differed from ours."[1] The point of departure was a celebrated novel of the same title by Bohdan Czeszko, with whom Wajda had occasionally collaborated, notably on the somewhat patchy screenplay of *Three Stories. A Generation,* which is still school reading in Poland, was in its time a book of historical as well as literary significance. Concerning a young man whose character and political thinking are moulded in the wartime resistance, it contained a strongly autobiographical streak: Czeszko had himself fought in the left-wing Underground associated with the communist Polish Workers Party. He belonged to a generation of young writers whose work drew inspiration from their Occupation experiences and who were bent on challenging the older generation. Almost all made a point of tracing the derivation of their attitudes, choices, and commitment to socialist ideology in their wartime biographies. Here lay their roots, the matrix of their identity. They also exerted a considerable influence on literature and, above all, on "literary life" in Poland in the Fifties and Sixties.

Although his background was different, Wajda belonged to this same generation, and almost everyone associated with the film was equally young and in some way at odds with the state of the cinema as he found it. "It was not only the director and his assistant," Wajda has said, "but all of us—the cameraman, the assistant cameraman, the composer, the author of the script, most of the actors—who were newcomers. . . . This was something new, based on different principles—it was a group of people who wanted to make a film which would speak their minds. We were out not only to articulate our ideological dispositions and our moral sentiments, but

17

also to demonstrate what we liked, what appealed to us, what we had failed to see in Polish films so far."[2] Roman Polański (seen in the opening episode of the film) has recalled: "For us it was a film of tremendous importance. The whole Polish cinema began with it. It was a marvellous experience. . . . The whole crew was very young. Wajda was very young, very sincere. We worked day and night. He believed in what he was doing—this was something utterly new in Poland (these were still the Stalinist years): the film was different, young."[3]

In 1954 Italian neo-realism was making a triumphant passage through Polish cinemas, and Wajda has acknowledged its influence. "As we saw it, the studio footage was only meant to round off what was shot on location. For the first time in a Polish film, you saw scenes played in the rain or under a cloudy sky; all this had, for aesthetic or technical reasons, previously been anathema."[4] Here, then, was a much more imaginative approach to *mise-en-scène* and the handling of actors—one, in short, which let in a breath of fresh air and blew away some of the cobwebs of the canons with which the Polish cinema had been complying. The generation which found its voice in this film was in the mainstream of things, and with a clearer sense than ever before of what it was about, determined to confront its predecessors in the spheres of technique, aesthetics, style. What of the content, the message of the film?

The story is set in Wola, a working class area of Warsaw, among a group of youngsters during the Occupation. The principal character is Stach (Tadeusz Łomnicki), first seen stealing coal from German military transports along with his mates from the Wola slums. Later he goes to work for a German firm where he finds—and joins—a left-wing Underground organisation in the making. There is, however, another group in the factory whose allegiances are to the non-communist Home Army (the resistance arm of the Polish Government-in-Exile in London) and which is engaged in some shady dealings with the Germans. The leader of Stach's group is a girl called Dorota (Urszula Modrzyńska), and they fall in love. One morning, after unexpectedly spending the night with her, he sneaks out to buy some bread and on his way back sees her being led away by the Gestapo. He is left alone with his comrades-in-arms. The film has a second protagonist, Jasio Krone (Tadeusz Janczar), a craftsman's son, highly-strung and vacillating, who at first holds aloof, but throws himself all the more whole-heartedly into the struggle when he eventually commits himself. On the run from the Germans after a relief operation in the Ghetto, he dodges into a stair-well and runs higher and higher up the steps till he

Tadeusz Łomnicki with Urszula Modrzyńska in A GENERATION

finds his way barred by an iron grille. Climbing on the bannisters, he leaps to his death.

On the face of it, the story appears to be fairly stereotyped. At the centre there is a character with the required hallmarks of the "positive hero": high-minded, uncompromising, dogged, with all the mandatory virtues and not a trace of doubts, complications or crises. Incidental detail also reveals, on the surface at any rate, a similar adherence to the directives of the time: for instance, the discrediting of the Home Army shown collaborating almost overtly with the Germans (one of the tenets of the early Fifties).

It is not enough to say that *A Generation* was made with such skill, feeling and power that it took these pitfalls in its stride. It deserves closer scrutiny to show where and how the shifting of its emphasis was brought about. Let

19

me touch only on the most salient point: the characterisation of the two protagonists. It is a fair guess that the inner world to which Wajda personally felt most attuned was that of Jasio Krone—edgy, troubled, bewildered, switching from one extreme to another, and ultimately tragic—and not with Stach, the dour proletarian not to be deflected from his chosen course. So, against all the logic of the screenplay, it is Jasio who dominates the film—and with him the themes which have wound their way through all of Wajda's work: the sense of bitter defeat ("the heroes of this film are the people who lose, not the ones who win"); the tragic nature of human destiny (the man who dies is the one who most wanted to live); and beleaguerment (Jasio's line of escape is cut off by a barrier which leaves suicide as the only alternative, a *motif* which recurs in *Kanal*).

This does not mean, however, that Stach is reduced to merely a cardboard figure, since he does undergo a certain metamorphosis. Wajda intended this—

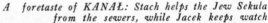

A foretaste of KANAŁ: Stach helps the Jew Sekula from the sewers, while Jacek keeps watch

and so did Tadeusz Łomnicki, one of Poland's most distinguished actors, who played the part. As he recalls: "It was easy to 'heroicise' this subject: we could have performed it violently, 'heroically,' which would for that matter have been equally truthful. However, we went about it differently: we wanted to create a style, a manner of performance, a portrayal of character, which would be more original: people heroic through their modesty. And that's the course we took. This is true both of the part of the girl, and also of mine."[5] True enough: the thing that struck anyone who saw the film in 1955 was that the "positive hero" was quite unlike the four-square, bronze-cast figures paraded for our greater admiration in those years. The response that Łomnicki's Stach courted with his rough edges, his straightforwardness, his unassuming manner, was, if anything, affection, even poignancy. He, too, was the focus of a tender love story that had never before been told so honestly and so movingly. After seeing *A Generation,* Ado Kyrou, author of the brilliant "Le surréalisme au cinéma," was moved to write: "As far as I know, Wajda is, apart from Lizzani, the only director since the days of *Blockade,* some of the Borzage films and the pre-war Soviet cinema who has integrated love into a revolutionary story or, more accurately, has not divorced those two primordial forces in man: love and revolt."[6] The theme of regenerating love was to become a recurrent *motif* in Wajda's films: twelve years after *Ashes and Diamonds* it appeared with redoubled intensity in *Landscape after the Battle.*

Wajda's distinctive language was already minted: the characteristics unveiled in *A Generation* are recognisable from his other films—the love of shock contrasts, the vehemence bordering on brutality. It had, in fact, moments of violence rarely seen in those days in the European cinema. At one point, Stach, as in Czeszko's novel, runs into a man outside a cemetery carrying an oddly bulging sack. He turns out to be a scavenger and the contents to be heads hacked off corpses for their gold fillings. This scene and others of a similar nature (like a fight between the two protagonists) were cut from the final version, but Wajda has always insisted that the film was built around a number of such sequences whose violence was intended to crystallise the narrative and its atmosphere. Equally evident in *A Generation* is a certain expressionist imagery. This is not so much a matter of an artist *manqué* straining after composition, elaborate harmony of shapes, outlines and light, as of a constant visual intensity, of images with dramatic bite: as the white trench-coat of the fleeing Jasio isolates him from the grey surroundings, the frame itself seems to be marking him down as doomed. This over-emphatic, highly-charged, often symbolic style of expression had critics already reaching for the adjective "baroque" with Wajda's very first film.

And yet, more perceptibly that in the later films, there is in *A Generation* a certain lightness of touch, a degree of ease in the *mise-en-scène,* a measure of relaxation in the acting. The film came over more like a captured fragment of reality than painfully re-created scenes from history—at all events that was the impression it gave when first released, so strong was the contrast with many of the Polish and foreign films then making the rounds. It is a curious paradox that when *Ashes* appeared in the mid-Sixties, it was charged by younger audiences with being laboured, operatic and monumental. Had Wajda changed, or the film-going frame of reference?

Wajda recalls that when *A Generation* was finished the state producer was at first less than enthusiastic. In an interview given to the French journal "Positif" he said that among the objections were the choice of a *lumpenproletariat* hero and, more seriously, the violence and brutality of certain scenes. It was, however, passed in the end and opened on January 25, 1955.

The reviews were attentive, but no more, apart from emphasising the appearance of an interesting new director. Wajda's old tutor, Antoni Bohdziewicz, wrote that at last "real life has been glimpsed on the screen instead of stale pap."[7] Otherwise the tone was generally cool, with far less excitement than might have been expected. One complaint persistently raised was that the film attempted to imitate neo-realism, thereby weaving Polish events into an alien emotional context. However, the main reason for the luke-warm reception seems to lie elsewhere. In an atmosphere of rapidly ensuing political change the film could have seemed too half-hearted a departure from the accepted canons in some of its assumptions and treatment of certain themes. On the other hand, conservatives might have been put out by the little resemblance it bore to the orthodox film it had at first promised to be.

Unfortunately, neither one side nor the other were able to see beyond the moods of the moment and recognise the abiding values of *A Generation*: the depth of its human concern and the freshness and power with which it is communicated. Nor did it dawn on them that from it would come an original artistic growth of great significance.

* * *

As soon as he had completed *A Generation,* Wajda made a short, *I Walk to the Sun (Idę ku słońcu),* at the Documentary Film Studios in Warsaw. Behind this rather high-flown title lay a documentary about a celebrated sculptor, Ksawery Dunikowski, who since the beginning of the century had been developing a monumental style of sculpture—brooding, dramatic, grandiloquent. He was regarded as the most distinguished living Polish sculptor—and with some justice, even if his style owed more to the spirit of the 1910s than the Fifties. No doubt it was this very strain of hyperbole and portentousness in his art that attracted Wajda. He introduced the sculptures and the artist himself, an old man with unbelievably expressive features, using suitably high-keyed contrasts: bright shafts of light piercing the darkness of the studio to pick out objects. Then came the most arresting sequence: shots of a set of sculptures on the theme of motherhood—figures of pregnant women—grouped on a beach drenched in sunlight as though to accentuate the innate ties between Dunikowski's art and nature, its drama and its majesty. The commentary came from the artist himself, whose language like his art followed the fashion of the early years of this century for the flowing, sonorous phrase:

"Man in the shackles of life, man in the service of life; I walk to the sun in quest of the mystery of being in the inspiration which gives birth to our consciousness, in the play of creative forces; I seek the mystery of being in conception, in a woman with child, in a new life, in the way it arises, in the way it is born from the old."

Tadeusz Janczar in his final flight up the stair-well

4. Between Scepticism and Enthusiasm—*Kanał*

THE TURN of 1956, when the tide of political change was still running high, found Wajda at work on *Kanał* ("Sewer"), adapted by Jerzy Stefan Stawiński from one of his own stories. Stawiński belongs to the same generation as the author of *A Generation,* Bohdan Czeszko, and like him bore witness to its ripening during the war, the background in his case being his experiences as a young officer in the underground Home Army which reached their climax in the Warsaw Rising of August 1944. This theme is the inspiration of his best writing. Well constructed, exact, semi-documentary, it attracted a number of the younger film-makers in the Fifties: Andrzej Munk's *Eroica,* his next film after *Man on the Track* and his best, Witold Lesiewicz's *The Deserter* (*Dezerter*) and Jerzy Passendorfer's *Answer to Violence* (*Zamach*) were all Stawiński stories. It was *Kanał,* however, which caused the greatest stir.

Stawiński's treatment of the events in which he had been directly involved was sober, balanced, and frankly sympathetic to the soldiers of the Home Army, though tempered by a streak of scepticism as to the purpose and price of their heroism. A certain critical attitude to the traditional image of Polish heroism forms an undercurrent to much of his fiction. It is revealing that this could be tailored equally smoothly to, at one extreme, a beady-eyed reappraisal of the heroic myth like Munk's *Eroica* and, at the other, an ingenuous panegyric like Passendorfer's *Answer to Violence.* Midway between the two lies *Kanał,* a singular blend of the affirmative and the critical.

It is for that reason one of Stawiński's most powerful pieces of writing, woven to a large extent from his own experiences: during the Rising, he fought in a battalion based in Mokotów, a southern area of Warsaw which was eventually cut off from the centre where the insurgents' main forces were grouped. The only line of withdrawal lay underground, through the sewers. It was a route taken by many thousands of people, mainly Home Army fighters, and Stawiński was one of them. The story and screenplay are a fictionalised account of this horrifying, subterranean trek, alternating between hope and despair, through a labyrinth bristling with German booby-traps and stinking of excrement—something of a contemporary vision of hell.

Opposite: Home Army fighters making for cover at the beginning of KANAŁ

*A wounded Tadeusz Janczar is borne to safety by Emil Karewicz after
immobilising one of the "Goliath" mini-tanks*

Certainly this was how the subject was seen by Wajda when, with *A
Generation* and acknowledgement of his promise under his belt, he began
production. The picture opens with a tracking shot of a company led by
Lieutenant Zadra (Wieńczysław Gliński) moving into the attack. Every so
often the camera pauses to zoom into a close-up of the faces while a commentary laconically recites their names and the odd characteristic. "This is
Halinka, the courier; leaving home she promised her mother she would
keep warm." The commentary ends with the words: "These are the last
hours of their lives. Mark them well!" At once the atmosphere of what is
to follow has been established. A sequence follows of typical episodes from
the Rising set in various moods ranging from carefree to grim. In some
that early eschatological note is echoed, as when one of the men rings his
wife (this is not stretching plausibility—by a quirk of circumstances phone
lines were still, despite the havoc, working across the battle lines) and hears

*Wieńczysław Gliński as the commander
seen prior to the descent into the sewers*

a voice at the other end call out in horror: "They're coming, they're here."

This "prologue" leads to the beginning of the main part of the film: the descent into the sewers. From here on it divides into three interlocking parts devoted to separate groups. The first of these, led by Mądry (Emil Karewicz), a daredevil in the time-honoured Polish style, includes Halinka and a demented composer; Halinka finally cracks up under the pressure and commits suicide. Eventually Mądry finds an exit and, dazzled after the murkiness of the sewers, climbs out straight into the midst of waiting German soldiers. Under a wall lie the bodies of executed prisoners and he kneels down among them. The second group consists of Stokrotka—"Daisy" (Teresa Iżewska)—and Korab (Tadeusz Janczar) who plod on through the filth, their spirits rising and falling, all the while talking of love, until they finally reach an outlet into the river, only to find it barred by an iron grille through which can be glimpsed a "normal" world beyond. The third

27

of the groups is led by Zadra, the officer who has the strongest doubts about the sense of the Rising and who is in a way the antithesis of Mądry ("Attacking tanks and planes with pistols and grenades? Will we never learn reason!"). He, a sergeant, a professional quartermaster, and another soldier become separated from the main body in the search for an exit, though Zadra is sure the rest are right behind. The soldier is killed, but Zadra and the sergeant are successful. When he discovers that the sergeant has been fooling him and that the company has been left far behind, Zadra shoots him on the spot and goes back into the sewers to look for his comrades.

In style the film is constructed as a steadily mounting crescendo. To quote from Wajda's own preliminary working notes:

"The picture must swell in time with the action of the story, and so the whole of the first part . . . ought to be kept in as documentary a style as possible: long takes, travelling shots, long shots, no close-ups. Part two: the

Kazimierz Kutz (one of Wajda's assistants) appears briefly (at left) as a deranged inhabitant of the sewers

Teresa Berezowska and Emil Karewicz

images intensify, flickering lighting (from the flames), close-ups, highlight the church by means of the charred statues, wounded. The Dante-esque descent into the sewers. Part three: the sewers. The descent and the first part normal, then, especially in the close-up scenes, a disturbing depth of focus (double exposure). The emergence from the sewers thoroughly jolting (colour perhaps?) and an uncanny establishing shot."[1]

Made with overpowering visual force, *Kanał* straddles a gulf between the realism of actual events with characters who are reasonably faithful portraits of the mentality and attitudes of the time, and an almost abstract vision of a sealed world whose inhabitants are doomed to extinction. Inevitably a parallel was drawn with Dante's "Inferno"—by Wajda himself as well as reviewers—and it is true that the film is permeated by a virtually unrelieved mood of despair, bitterness and resignation. The whole structure is pivoted on the idea that there is no way out, no hope, no chance of deliverance. As in Dante there is only a succession of narrowing circles of torment. What a contrast with *A Generation* with its variations of tone, its rays of hope, its surges of *joie de vivre* intermingling with the intimations of death! How are we to explain this violent switch?

The simplest answer—and the interpretation once favoured—would be to say that, weary of the *clichés* of the preceding period with its forced optimism and sentimentality, Wajda decided to make a clean break; it was in other words a superficial, purely aesthetic reaction. There were grounds for drawing this conclusion since there were a number of films around at the time which were just such a formal rebuke to the "schematism" of the early Fifties. All they did was simply reverse the old picture of life: mindless optimism turned into mindless pessimism, good into bad, hero into villain, and so on. It was, in effect, the same mixture as before, but with the *clichés* inverted. The evolution of cinema between *A Generation* in 1955 and *Kanał* in 1957 was, however, quite another thing. Wajda's treatment of the Warsaw Rising and the retreat through the sewers had a definite and deliberate historical and social edge.

One must bear in mind that the events in question were charged with controversy. The outbreak of the Rising on August 1, 1944 was ordered by the Home Army leaders in agreement with the Government-in-Exile in London, but no clear understanding was made with the command of the approaching Soviet armies. These were just east of Warsaw and its bridges were being used by the Germans to rush troops across the river. Caught on the wrong foot by the Rising, they were at first driven out of large areas of the city by the Poles. However, deadlock was reached on the Soviet front, and a war of attrition was mounted against the insurgents which continued for several weeks. Gradually the remorseless German assault gained effect, and insurgents were forced to withdraw, first from Mokotów in the south, and then from the Old Town quarter in the centre. Finally, after two months' fighting, the Home Army command surrendered. Warsaw was evacuated and those buildings still left standing systematically demolished (on Hitler's express order) by German sapper squads during the course of November and December 1944. The price paid for the Rising was several hundred thousand dead and the immolation of the homes of over a million people.

Despite the fearful toll, or perhaps for that very reason, the unbelievable heroism of so many thousands of young men and women became engraved on the public mind. The Warsaw Rising of 1944 quietly passed into national

Characters under pressure

history as yet another gallant chapter, as one more tragic episode which, though an idle sacrifice, nevertheless gave birth to a legend. Officially, however, this aspect of the Rising was played down in the early Fifties and the accent put instead on the devious motives of the Home Army command and the Government-in-Exile. There was, therefore, a distinct rift between the official account and popular sentiment, between the political facts of life and folk consciousness. Inevitably the legend of the tragic Rising spread to ever wider circles, and a measure of complexity arose from the contradiction between the honour and bravery of the mass of the Home Army and the suspect ends to which they were put. Thus, the Rising became an issue not only of historical interest, but also with a sharp and pregnant contemporary dimension.

Wajda's film was the first after the political watershed of 1956 to air this emotive subject before the general public. He did not, however, intend

A glimpse of the outside world. Emil Karewicz, at right

it to be some kind of message film, or indictment of the men responsible for the tragedy of the Rising. "The only thing that may strike one," he noted at the time, "is the absence of one element, namely 'force of circumstances' (let us leave it at that, in inverted commas) which precipitated the drama; but I can see no way of presenting this on the screen until the problem has first been sorted out by the historians on the basis of the evidence. Anything that I might suggest going on my own conjectures would be merely nebulous hypothesis."[2] Wajda preferred—and his reasons must be taken at their face value—not to go into the political, social or even strategic context beyond the immediate drama of his cast of characters. He wished to tell the story as three small groups traversing the circles of hell. No more.

But even Dante's "Inferno" had undertones of political pamphleteering, Wajda was hard-pressed in his aim. The already cited "Notebook" contains the following entry for January 26, 1956 when work on the film was just starting: "The credits are preceded by shots of uhlans galloping into the attack. These are the uhlans of Samosierra, Rokitna and those who rode down tanks in 1939." The cavalry charges referred to—at Samosierra during Napoleon's Spanish campaign, at Rokitna in 1915, and in 1939 (the subject of *Lotna* later)—are all bywords for acts of courage as futile as they were desperate. Such an introduction to a film about the Warsaw Rising could only signify that it had been the latest (perhaps the last?) of a string of historical follies. Though Wajda eventually thought better of this pre-credit sequence, the idea was still there. "Future generations will honour us," says one of the soldiers, to which Zadra, the man who seems to speak most for the author of the screenplay, replies: "Yes, the Polish way!" and adds angrily: "Will we never learn reason?" Here we have a definite comment "on Polish heroism," present no doubt in Stawiński's original, an implicit critique of "Polishness," the lack of political and social common sense, the propensity for disproportionately high sacrifices. According to this line of thinking, national history was one long chain of foolhardiness. Far from being new, this idea could have seemed thoroughly dated in the Fifties. However, it is worth tracing its pedigree since it has a bearing on the historical and philosophical implications both of all Wajda's films and of the whole of what came to be called the "Polish film school." In the second half of the Nineteenth century, after the latest of the national insurrections had been defeated in 1863, there arose a school of historical and social thought which propagated a similar interpretation of Polish history with a similar appeal to reason: discard fruitless heroics and concentrate on the spade-work of building the foundations of economic life, education and culture. It may be wondered why this philosophy should suddenly, half a century later, have acquired a new lease of life. The answer is that immediately after the War, when the ravaged country was struggling to re-define its economic and intellectual position, the watchwords of political common sense were loudly invoked as the only suitable option; at the same time, romanticism, heroism, the "spirit of the ages" were denounced as the root causes of the most recent disasters—both the *débâcle* of 1939 and the tragedy of the Warsaw Rising. Thus, round about 1956, when the idea of making a film about the Rising materialised, two attitudes to this event (and others like it) were current in the public mind: scepticism as to the sense of what seemed yet another heroic though misguided episode in Polish history, and whole-hearted and unqualified acclamation of the legend of the valiant, indomitable young Poles.

And Wajda? I think that it is only against this background that one can understand the certain moral and historical ambiguity (or even confusion) which lurks in almost all the films he has made about the past—from *Kanał* and *Lotna* to *Ashes* in 1965. The point is that the sort of sceptical musings about Polish history evident in *Kanał* seem to sit very uneasily on the romantic, sensual style which has been Wajda's natural idiom from the outset. In contrast to Andrzej Munk who was not going against his own grain—tart, rational, alert to intellectual paradoxes—when he intimated (also with the help of Stawiński) his national scepticism in *Eroica*, Wajda has always been predisposed to emotional flights, frenzied romantic hyperbole, and larger-than-life portrayal of characters. The language used in *Kanał*, rhetorical, vehement, full of contrasts and dramatic visual effects, inflated its characters to heroic dimensions. With all the stops pulled out, the scepticism latent in the screenplay and scattered around the film could hardly make itself heard.

A Polish critic, Krzysztof Teodor Toeplitz, crystallised the problem when he wrote: "Like all authors approaching this subject, Wajda has succumbed

Tadeusz Gwiazdowski, Wieńczysław Gliński and Stanisław Mikulski

to certain pressures. On the one hand there was the rational pressure against delivering an apologia for the Rising and, on the other, the emotional pressure against undertaking a merciless criticism of the Rising. The film stopped halfway."[3]

The reception of the film in Poland—far stormier than in the case of *A Generation*—centred around this curious dilemma. It is typical of Wajda's films, and of the films of this period in general, that they have triggered off large public controversies. The point at issue was vindication or condemnation not only of an issue of national history, but also of certain contemporary moral and political attitudes. It is no wonder that passions were aroused.

Some people had been looking forward to a sublime and stirring work *à la* Racine, but *Kanał* turned out quite different "This whole Warsaw," wrote one disgruntled critic, "its whole Rising wallows in filth, in the gutters of history," adding that Wajda had gone further than the anti-

The face of disillusionment: Wieńczysław Gliński about to return to the sewers

Polish politicians, impugning what had been a noble, spontaneous and popular struggle and investing it with a tragic absurdity and pointlessness.[4] In another paper a critic wrote that "the common people of Warsaw were not the bunch of desperadoes that Wajda has made of them."[5]

Nor was *Kanal* to the liking of the adherents of the now shop-worn formula for optimistic films with carefully-balanced social and political proportions: on every count—aesthetic, moral, political—it was poles apart, desperate, one-sided, tragic. Yet the critic of the official daily "Trybuna ludu," Aleksander Jackiewicz, wrote: "Maybe *Kanal* will mark the beginning of the truth being told about history, about ourselves, about a whole generation. Perhaps it will prove to be art as warning, art as purgation, a triumph of the heroism of life over the heroism of death?"[6] Jackiewicz placed the emphasis on the sceptical note in the film, its confrontation with the legend of the Rising, and by and large this was how other reviewers hailed *Kanal* as a landmark in Polish cinema.

The *première* took place on April 20, 1957 and three weeks later, when outrage and enthusiasm were still in full cry in Poland, the film collected a directing award at Cannes. It was the first encounter between Wajda's cinema and a non-Polish audience.

5. Polish Encounters with the Revolution
—*Ashes and Diamonds*

WAJDA'S THIRD FILM, *Ashes and Diamonds* (*Popiół i diament*), is not only his most important work but also the supreme achievement of post-war Polish cinema. Shot at the turn of 1957, it was based on a novel by Jerzy Andrzejewski published in the Forties—one of the literary landmarks of its period. These two dates, and the ten-year interval, are significant: Andrzejewski's book sprang from the emotional and political atmosphere of the first years after the war, when the shock of Occupation was followed by the shock of Liberation as a new social framework, founded on a different system of values, began to be hammered out amid the wreckage. The novel graphically evoked a widespread longing to have done with internal strife and re-forge a nationwide sense of common purpose no matter how great the difference in recent biographies and one-time political allegiances. This message, decried as false in the early Fifties, acquired a fresh currency after 1956. This was the moment when the notion of making a screen version of *Ashes and Diamonds* took shape.

It is the spring of 1945, the day after the liberation of a provincial town. The nightmare of the occupation has come to an end, but no one is yet quite certain of the new dawn. On the outskirts of the town, two gunmen, Maciek (Zbigniew Cybulski) and Andrzej (Adam Pawlikowski), ambush a jeep in which Szczuka (Wacław Zastrzeżyński), the Party secretary due to take charge of the new communist authorities, is supposed to be arriving. When it is discovered that the wrong men have been killed, Maciek's Underground organisation orders him to make another attempt. In the meantime both the assassin and his prospective victim have taken rooms, practically next door to one another, in the same seedy hotel, which now becomes the focal point of the drama. Maciek has a brief affair, hurried, unexpected, out-of-the-ordinary, with one of the Monopol's barmaids (Ewa Krzyżewska). In the reception rooms army and civic brass, hangers-on, and local worthies gather for a banquet to celebrate the liberation. Next door, in the hotel restaurant, there is junketing of another kind: a haphazard crowd of people privately toasting the end of the occupation, some filled with dire forebodings, others hoping for the best. Daybreak draws near: Maciek's night with Krystyna ends and the victory dinner breaks up. The time has come

Confusion after the mishandled assassination attempt

to carry out his orders: he leaves the hotel and shoots the strolling Szczuka who lurches forward and collapses into his arms. As Maciek bolts through the streets of the town, the revellings in the Monopol draw to a close: a dawn *polonaise* to cap the patriotic songs, the dancers rapt and glassy-eyed as though transfixed by anticipation of what is in store. As the party fizzles out, Maciek, shot by chance by some soldiers, thrashes in foetus-like convulsions on a rubbish heap in his death agony. The tragedy has run its course in a matter of hours: when the gunmen's first shots were fired it was afternoon; when Maciek dies on the rubbish heap, it is early morning.

At first glance we have, therefore, a story of violence and love, deftly plotted and compulsively told: the assassin balks at his assignment, falters, thinks of backing out, but in the end goes through with it and is struck down shortly afterwards. At one level, *Ashes and Diamonds* is indeed a straightforward, suspenseful thriller; but there is more to its interest than that. At another level (just as immediately obvious) it has a dimension of high tragedy: as in ancient drama Maciek is the prisoner of a fate he is powerless to escape. At the very moment that he discovers, apparently for the first time, a love which regenerates and reprieves and has a foretaste of the flavour of happiness, he is summoned to kill and be killed. The unity of time and place accentuate this tragic note.

Deep down, however, *Ashes and Diamonds* has a broader meaning, sometimes missed by non-Polish audiences. The date of these fateful hours between the afternoon of one day and the morning of the next must be held in mind: it is the first day after the war, the first day of a new age. In this space of time it is more than the course of a single romance and single killing that reaches its breaking-point. The lives of these people and their nation stand at a crossroads between two eras. The occupation is over, but through those harrowing years of bloodshed, hardship and struggle, men's minds had been too pre-occupied with the necessities of battle and survival to give much thought to the exact shape of post-war realities. Now, all at once, they have been pitched face to face with ones which, like lava from an erupting volcano, are only just beginning to solidify. And it was a mighty upheaval, a change not just of government, but of the whole political and social structure, of the class system to which the country had been accustomed for many centuries. In this melting-pot there was to be fused a new class, social, and national identity. A challenge was also being made to the nation's traditional moral and social hierarchies, beliefs and myths, and a different mentality, way of life and ideals propagated in their place. Long-suppressed aspirations broke through to the surface; so did apprehensions. This first day marked the onset, therefore, of a dramatic process which was to continue for many years.

This is what gave the film the immediacy of impact which it sustained for so long; and why, too, it was at once suspected of anachronism: what year was it pretending to be about, 1945 or 1958? The truth is that the strength of *Ashes and Diamonds* lies in the way it caught certain momentous historical phenomena which appeared for the first time in 1944, were still in evidence in 1958, and to some extent still linger. It has, therefore, all the ingredients of a national epic, showing individual destinies being re-shaped in the turmoil of a great *débâcle*.

When *Ashes and Diamonds* went into release—the *première* took place on October 3, 1958—everyone, audiences and critics alike, realised that it was one of those films that come along only exceptionally in the history of the cinema. It moved even a critical reviewer to write: "It is a spellbinding, stirring work which imposes its own view of the world. You may—as I do—disagree with it, but there is no denying its stature."[1] Basically, there were two complaints. One was with the general spirit of hopelessness and fatalism which emanates from the film: "Strange laws govern this visionary world of phantoms, obsessions and distortions . . . It suggests some kind of requiem in the presence of a horrifying death." The other—and it was one taken up by most Polish critics and dogged Wajda for many years to come—was a charge of excessive ornateness, of indulging in effects for their own sake; Wajda's art was, in short, pronounced "baroque," though in a few cases the adjective was meant as a compliment.

The public discussion provoked by *Ashes and Diamonds* generated a great deal of heat and was not confined to the professional critics—one of the more interesting comments came from Maria Dąbrowska, a distinguished writer not accustomed to sounding off on mere matters of the moment. A good indication of the temperature of the debate was the unconcealed *pique* of the leading critic Zygmunt Kałużyński, who seemed to take the expressions of acclaim as a personal affront: "Its enthusiastic reception is very telling from the pedagogical and sociological point of view. Gun-toting punks like Maciek, now doping themselves on the subtleties of Western fashions, were to be found on either side of the barricades: do their raves over the film signify self-criticism or self-glorification, or have they detected nothing but a caricature of themselves?"[2]

The heart of the matter lay in the social and political implications of *Ashes and Diamonds,* and these were traced to the presentation and confrontation of its two key figures: Maciek the assassin and Szczuka the representative of the new government. To understand the dimensions of the argument, one point must be comprehended: it was assumed, in both corners of the ring, that they were typical, emblematic figures, the conclusion being that the characterisation of Szczuka related not only to the man himself but also to the political force for which he stood; and the same applied to Maciek. This was why so much was made of the fact that the "representative" of the authorities is an old man, tired, soured, a little lackadaisical, while the "representative" of the anti-communist Underground is young, dynamic, captivating and unforgettable in every gesture and glance from behind his dark glasses. The critic of the official daily "Trybuna ludu," who took the side of the film, wrote: "On their subject [Maciek and Szczuka] we have heard criticism which can be summed up in the accusation that the communists in this film are not presented strongly enough to be an equal

*Zbigniew Cybulski with Ewa Krzyżewska during their night
"in the seedy hotel"*

force in the conflict, that the weakness in the drawing of Szczuka even di-
minishes the drama of Maciek which has been precipitated by the victory
of the communists in Poland. These objections seem unfair . . . It is
Maciek who is the hero of the film and the subject of the conflict, Szczuka
only its object."[3] A similar line in defence of the portrayal of Maciek was
taken by Roman Szydłowski: "[The likes of Maciek] were cruel and un-
thinkingly ruthless, but they were also tragically adrift, hopelessly trapped
in their blind obedience and their hatred of the new government, communism
and the Soviet Union drummed into them for years . . . I understood [the
film] quite unambiguously to be about the wrong done a generation of
youngsters who died abjectly and in a squalid cause when they might have
lived for the good of their country and themselves."[4]

Let us, however, take a closer look at these two figures. Even if we dis-
count the notion of their political "representativeness," it is still in their

provenance that the key to the film's meaning lies. Szczuka, the revolutionary fated to be murdered, is an ageing, somewhat stolid man, possibly exhausted by the long years of political struggle (there is a suggestion that he also fought in the Spanish Civil War); in him lies a certain tolerant view of the surrounding events, and he is, in any case, himself involved in the whole dramatic tangle of Polish dilemmas, misunderstandings and cross-purposes: his son, left in the custody of his ex-wife, joined the Home Army as one might expect and has turned up in the same anti-communist Underground as Maciek. Thus caught up in the convolutions of the political situation of Poland in 1945, Szczuka views the turbulent new world not with the eyes of an energetic, robust and uncomplex-ridden Party organiser and outsider, but of a man who knows that, no matter what, everything must once again be started anew—but with whom and against whom?

Maciek, in contrast, was in the pro-London Home Army, fought in the Warsaw Rising (and may, for all we know, have trudged through the sewers along with Zadra, Korab and Mądry) and after the liberation threw in his lot with the anti-communist guerrillas less, one suspects, from conviction than from a sense of duty and loyalty to his commanding officers. He proceeds with the execution even though he has come, in the course of the preceding night, to have a glimmer of the enormity of the act. Despite the trappings of the late Fifties in his appearance—the dark glasses which serve as a kind of mask—he belongs to the generation which grew up under the Occupation, and is one of those people whom the writer Tadeusz Borowski called "contaminated by death" because they had seen and experienced too much. The love he finds in these brief hours regenerates him, crystallises all his honourable qualities and restores an attachment to life which had been drained out of him.

The stage behind these two contrasted figures is filled with the motley fauna of the hotel, of the welcoming and farewell dinners. There are people from the old Establishment now making their final exit with a sense of defeat but with *élan,* to the strains of an Ogiński *polonaise* called "Adieu à la patrie." And others who mean to swim with the new tide and, swallowing their deep-seated misgivings, enter the race for power. At dawn all join in the *polonaise,* heady with drink but tense, alert, aware that they are crossing a watershed of history.

Meanwhile, the corpse of the communist Szczuka is already stiffening on

Opposite: the climactic party in full swing. Bogumił Kobiela as Drewnowski

the pavement outside and his killer dying in convulsions on a rubbish heap. Can it be that these two men, who fell into each other's arms in a paradoxical embrace at the moment of assassination, are in fact brothers, regardless of all adversaries, careerists and dogmatists? Such an appeal for solidarity was implicit in Andrzejewski's novel, and it is echoed in the film.

Certainly there is no suggestion in *Ashes and Diamonds* of hostility towards the revolution which followed (as some imputed), or even of scepticism as to the sense of the upheaval of 1945. It only emphasises the great drama of these changes without glossing over the bitter and sometimes tragic predicaments they involved. The film shows this encounter with the new social system not according to the standard formula of socialist cinema of the time, but according to the realities of a specific date in a specific country—Spring 1945, Poland. At the time of production, in 1957–8, such a simple assertion of specific differences had the freshness of discovery. I think this may also be the reason why so many strands from the Polish artistic tradition found their way into the film—and the novel before it. Certainly its inspiration can be traced to Nineteenth-century Romanticism, which has been the most fruitful vein in Polish literature.

Ashes and Diamonds contains clear links with that century: to Norwid, an expatriate poet and thinker of genius, from one of whose verses its title is taken; to Juliusz Słowacki and his drama; and, most deliberately, to the turn-of-the-century Kraków writer and painter, Stanisław Wyspiański, the most brilliant successor to this heritage. His *The Wedding* (still one of the most vibrant plays in the Polish theatrical canon) is a great parable of the nation's situation in his day; it contains an uncanny, riveting scene, repeated almost literally in *Ashes and Diamonds*, when at dawn, towards the end of a country wedding, the guests—bemused? dazed? stupefied?—shuffle slowly and monotonously through a grotesque dance which anticipates some fateful change in their lives and their country. It is Wajda's favourite play, and he has now, 14 years after *Ashes and Diamonds*, filmed it as it stands.

The Polish literary tradition makes itself felt in more ways, however, than in quotes from the classics or allusions to various authors. The film bears the stamp of a certain attitude towards the individual, the community, and the nation, of a certain logic in the approach to human destiny

Opposite: aftermath and dawn, with Ewa Krzyżewska

Cybulski "thrashes in foetus-like convulsions"

planted by Polish literature in the Nineteenth century (a time of servitude and persistent, savagely-suppressed rebellion). In the interpretation of the great poets of the age—Norwid, Mickiewicz, Słowacki, Krasiński—Poland assumed a distinct identity: lofty, magnificent, innately Romantic, she was seen as hero, sage, saint and, above all, martyr. In its extreme version, the doctrine of Polish Messianism, she became the Christ of nations, crucified to redeem them. Obviously, given such a point of view, the tragedy of the corporate destiny placed the individual's beyond hope: collective martyrdom implied individual martyrdom. Men were merely pawns on the chess-board of History, moved by invisible forces. Poland and the Poles were treated by this literature in a key of emotional extremes: from wild enthusiasm to furious condemnation, from gushing love to demented rage.

It was in a situation such as this that poetry, literature and art began to play a remarkable role. "The artist of Polish Romanticism," none other than Wajda himself has said, "was not someone who fulfilled himself entirely in the fabric of his art—in poetry, painting or sculpture. He tried to outdo himself, and the historical situation came to his aid. He was something more than an author; he was the conscience of the nation, a prophet, and social institution. Poland in the Nineteenth century was a country shorn of normal institutions: power, government, parliament, political life, public opinion. It was the poets who did duty for all these institutions. In a sense it was, of course, an act of usurpation."[5]

The reason I quote Wajda's own comment on this matter is that, in spite of entirely different historical circumstances, the artistic current which he helped to launch—the "Polish Film School"—and his own *oeuvre* in particular, represent a complete commitment to such a mission of art. Moreover, his treatment of human fortunes and the emotional climate of all his films are both very much in the spirit of the tradition in question, and nowhere is this more eloquently demonstrated than in *Ashes and Diamonds*.

6. Caricature or Panegyric?—*Lotna*

IN THE AUTUMN of 1958, as the argument over *Ashes and Diamonds* raged on, Wajda and his regular cameraman, Jerzy Lipman, were shooting *Lotna* in the region of the River Narew outside Warsaw. It is a curious film: considered a misfire not only by many critics but even, apparently, by Wajda himself, it is nevertheless an extremely telling chapter in his work, strongly marked by the imprint of his sensibilities and very much a product of his universe.

The screenplay was adapted by Wajda and Wojciech Żukrowski from a story by the latter, a short and succinct piece of writing about a magnificent mare called Lotna which enthrals the men of a cavalry unit with her looks but brings misfortune to each of her successive owners. Żukrowski's racy and realistic prose vividly captured the atmosphere of the tragic, beautiful autumn of 1939, but was confined basically to the theme of this jinx. The narrative, psychological and historical substance of this terse tale had, therefore, to be filled out by the script, which took a long time to assemble

LOTNA: a characteristically detailed Wajda set

and underwent endless revision and alteration. In the end the film was, in fact, largely improvised.

On the screen it still looks, at first glance, like the story of a beautiful white mare called Lotna, the gift of an old man to the commanding officer of a cavalry troop during the invasion of Poland in September 1939. She is first seen standing at the head of his bed like a faithful retainer waiting for the death of her master. As the film proceeds, and in time with the course of the September campaign, the soldiers who acquire Lotna are killed one by one. The first is the captain; the mare then passes to a subaltern who meets and falls in love with a girl, marries her in a bizarre, hurried ceremony, and shortly afterwards loses his life. In the end a lieutenant and a sergeant are the only ones left alive. Finally, as the September campaign draws to a close and the sunny autumn of 1939 ends,

Lotna herself dies when she breaks a leg and has to be shot; as though suddenly robbed of the strength to fight on, the two soldiers part company and wander off into the distance, stooped and leaning on sticks.

The story is told in a loose-knit, leisurely, almost off-hand manner, events following one another desultorily and at random. On closer inspection, however, there emerge three levels, three parallel axes around which everyone and everything revolves. First, and much more prominent than the background it ostensibly is, we have a panorama of the fighting in 1939—attack and counter-attack, desperate stands, an army on the retreat—and the havoc it has wreaked—panicking civilians, streams of refugees, somnolent villages jolted awake by the crash of artillery, country houses milling with troops, make-shift hospitals, hurried funerals.

The second level is devoted to the group of cavalrymen: captain, lieutenant, subaltern and sergeant. As characters, they are sketchily drawn, little more than two-dimensional silhouettes. Though actors in the tragedy, they seem hardly aware of what has overtaken them and are nothing like the anguished, hysterical figures of *Kanał*. Nor does any sense of bitter defeat appear to haunt these simple, clean-limbed heroes with their Boys' Own appeal. The fabric of slender incident between them and the romance of the subaltern and schoolteacher are similarly ingenuous. "Everything here," observed one critic aptly, "is straightforward, picturesque, dashing—and tragic."[1]

Finally, there is the last level of the film, the pivot of the Żukrowski original and the peg on which the various strands of the film were supposed to hang: the story of Lotna. At one level, she is just an ordinary white cavalry mare, apart from her exceptional beauty; at another, she is a symbol of a dying world, a harbinger (perhaps agent?) of misfortune. She also serves as a touchstone of men's characters, of their uprightness and patriotism; for, although the human relationships in *Lotna* are not examined in any great depth, attitudes to the mare are limned out in detail.

The film moves from level to level, but this does not seem to aid its flow and rhythm. The narration is jerky and rambling, and its emphases are not consistent. "I feel," Wajda has said, "that there was some kind of discord between what I wanted to do and the story I chose as the basis of the screenplay. When I look back on the film now, I believe a different idea might have worked: Don Quixote. If only I'd hit on it right away: the story of a cavalryman, the last cavalryman, roving through the savage world of contemporary war with his squire. If someone like that (and not a Polish cavalryman) had attacked a tank, everything would have looked

49

different. The film would have been more truthful, more profound and closer to us. At all events it would have been more European and less provincial."[2] Be that as it may, *Lotna* certainly lacks some such controlling idea to smoothe its progress. Would the theme of a contemporary Don Quixote have been the answer? One wonders.

For all that, *Lotna* remains pure Wajda: if an anthology of Wajda's style were ever to be compiled, here would be the *locus classicus*. It may have been the thinness of the script and the absence of a firm narrative structure which led Wajda to give vent to a highly personal idiom far removed from any literary model. It is a language of great visual intensity which owes much to a certain type of painting he came to admire while still at art school, one which combines minute attention to reality with the shock effect of gruesome or absurd detail. This style, which has affinities both with Nineteenth-century naturalism where it borders on *kitsch* and with the surrealism of the Twenties and Thirties, also seems close to that of Andrzej Wróblewski, a Kraków painter who met a tragic death and whom Wajda encountered at the outset of his career: Wróblewski's pictures contained subjects like tables with human legs or people standing in the most ordinary poses—but headless. The strange creatures glimpsed in *Lotna*— the expiring fish in the foreground of the love scene, the slit bodies of animals and people—are part of the same currency.

At the same time, for want of literary momentum, Wajda's *penchant* for symbolic imagery was given more rein than ever. The meanings that the situations, characters and dialogue were too weak to convey had to be emphasised by eloquent gestures and objects: a stuffed eagle on fire in a schoolroom (the eagle is the national emblem: Poland is burning); a snow-white handkerchief wiping the blood from a sword blade (white and red: the Polish colours); red rowanberries caught in a trooper's stirrups (drops of blood); a sabre slashing at a tank's gun barrel (the absurdity of such an attack); a bride's veil caught on a coffin (life and death); coffins in an attic filled with apples (death and life); the stick, like a pilgrim's staff, on which the hero limps off at the end (walking into a long, homeless exile); and, the supreme image of all, the scenery of a typical "golden Polish autumn," the season of the year regarded as the most beautiful in Poland. In the early scenes, when there is still hope, the landscape has a rich, lush colour which gradually turns drab and brown and fades away amid withered, leafless trees: the end of autumn, the end of heroes, the end of Poland.

It is not only the language of *Lotna* that is highly personal; the theme itself must also have been very close to Wajda's heart. Remember: "I grew

Bożena Kurowska with the horse

up in a cavalry barracks"; ". . . gun carriages drawn by three pairs of horses . . hurtling in at a gallop." Even so, he wanted (as in *Kanal*) to strike an objective balance between condemning the crassness of the generals and the reckless bravado of the men, and building a monument to them. "Despite appearances, I do not regard this film as a settling of accounts with the past," he told a reporter in October 1958 on the set of *Lotna*. "All I want is to stir audiences, because that is the easiest way of getting through to them. I want to say goodbye to a certain noble national tradition and I think this should make it a very Polish film."[3] It was not, therefore, Wajda's purpose either to caricature or to eulogise the past, but in spite (or, more likely, because) of this, *Lotna* suffers from the same confusion as *Kanal:* it is both travesty and encomium. As Zbigniew Florczak neatly stated in a discussion printed in a film weekly, Wajda "resembles an artist in love with his own caricature."[4] I am positive, however, that there was no element of calculation in this. On the contrary, if Wajda blew hot and

51

The painter's eye: an interior from LOTNA

cold, it was from surrendering to the pull of the conflicting emotions triggered by the date September 1939.

This ambiguity again incensed the critics and public, especially as *Lotna* was, like *Kanal,* the first Polish film about a tragic episode of history which some regarded with bitterness, anger and resentment and others with tearful sentiment and enthusiasm. Wajda pleased neither. And so there was another flurry of argument and recrimination.

However, there was a difference from the reception of *Ashes and Diamonds,* which even its opponents had to concede was outstanding cinema. *Lotna,* in contrast, was found by most critics to be full of faults: fustian, mannered, overloaded with symbolism, bordering on bad taste in its mixture of *naïveté* and violence. "Surrealism or Kitsch," "A Cavalry Nightmare,"

"The Poetry of Props" are a sample of the review titles. One writer called it, literally, "a pseudo-apocalyptic vision of a maniacal-obsessional nature," and another protested that it was "a picture of soldiers who let a horse obscure the cause of Poland; a picture of a group of inhuman and moronic friends awaiting their own death."

As can be seen it was not only the message, but also the style of *Lotna* that came under fire. Among the few critics who did not join in this chorus was Zygmunt Kałużyński, in the weekly "Polityka," who had delivered such a furious broadside against *Ashes and Diamonds* but now discovered a measure of greatness in Wajda, arguing that it was only in *Lotna* that the surrealist elements dotted around his films had at last been made to cohere: "This paradox can be explained by the moral of *Lotna:* it is in its way a cinematic epitaph to a dying world, and accordingly everything in it that is monstrous becomes a kind of symbolic elegy to the historical anachronism that now arouses our astonishment. Surrealism is the style of a civilisation in defeat, and so, strangely enough, it seems here to accord with the theme."[5]

The symbols of life and death are to the forefront in LOTNA

7. The Next Generation—*Innocent Sorcerers*

WITH THE ARRIVAL of 1960 Wajda had four films behind him, all connected with the war; the cinemas, meanwhile, had long been full of other pictures from the "Polish school" which also described in various keys and with mixed success similar Occupation dramas of a generation now approaching its forties. There were signs that the subject was beginning to wear thin: a *new* generation, which had only a brief memory of the war and the moral problems of the first days of peace, was now finding its feet in the country's life, and it was one whose mind was almost entirely shaped by the new conditions of post-war Poland. What were its particular pre-occupations and dilemmas?

The idea of making a film about these successors to the generation of veterans (or "Columbuses," as they were called—after the title of a popular novel by Roman Bratny) was a very natural one. The script was written by the author of *Ashes and Diamonds,* Jerzy Andrzejewski, in collaboration with a budding poet, Jerzy Skolimowski. The one brought to it the authority of a seasoned artist, the other a first-hand knowledge of the environment. For the first time this was an original screenplay—a point of some interest, since until then all Wajda's films had been adaptations of novels, in the tailoring of which he had played a prominent part. In this case he shot the film much as written, the script determining its style as well as content.

Although most of the writing seems to have been done by Andrzejewski, the contribution of Skolimowski was by no means token (hovering in the wings was also Roman Polański, limbering up for his own *début*). In fact, Skolimowski, as well as Polański, was shortly to break in on the scene with films which became highlights of Polish cinema in the mid-Sixties: Polański's *Knife in the Water* (*Nóż w wodzie*), co-scripted by Skolimowski, and Skolimowski's own *Distinguishing Marks—None* (*Rysopis*), *Walkover* and *Barrier* (*Bariera*). These works broached psychological, moral and social problems which had not previously been aired in Polish films: the concerns of a generation unscarred by wartime memories, ordeals and ideological quandaries, shaped by the present and rooted in the contemporary system, but nevertheless finding adjustment painful. No one needed to be told about the problems of adaptation experienced by the generation of *Ashes*

Opposite: Krystyna Stypułkowska as Pelagia

Tadeusz Łomnicki as the happy-go-lucky Bazyli

and Diamonds, so exhaustively portrayed in the cinema; but to learn that
the succeeding one, whose lives seemed untroubled, was having the same
sort of trouble was at first startling. This was what Skolimowski helped
to communicate in *Innocent Sorcerers* (*Niewinni czarodzieje*) and later in
Knife in the Water, but it appeared most tellingly in his own films: in
Distinguishing Marks—None, where he showed the difficulties, aggravated
by immature love, of coming to terms with the existing social institutions;
in *Walkover,* where we have a first, reluctant gesture of reconciliation and
a cautious, petulant inching towards acceptance of the need to find one's
place in life; and in *Barrier,* a fierce challenge to conformism, or rather
the temptation of conformism, which is stronger in a stabilised society.

But to return to 1960: *Innocent Sorcerers* was the first probe into the
psychology and *mores* of the post-war generation. Its theme was the damage
done by affecting a pose in personal relationships, the paralysing of authen-
tic responses and emotions and personality in general. This form of self-

Krystyna Stypułkowska

disguise was diagnosed as an ailment of the young. The film is set in Warsaw and centres on a young man, with a blonde rinse, named Bazyli (Tadeusz Łomnicki), whom we first see listening to a tape of a woman's incoherent but suggestive murmurs recorded the night before, while another girl tries to catch his attention outside. A sports doctor and jazz fan, he leads a fairly happy-go-lucky existence taking each day as it comes. This particular one brings him a new encounter: a girl (Krystyna Stypułkowska) equally sharp as himself, and quick to expose his lies, thoughts and embarassments. When they are left alone in his room there begins a night-long *tête-à-tête* or, to be more accurate, a psychological sparring match full of muted clashes, needlings and put-downs, momentary misunderstandings, anticipations of the inevitable and counterploys. Both are play-acting, feeling out their partner (or adversary), donning a new mask, striking another pose. These sly manoeuvres are carried out without any commitment of their real selves; it is a cut-and-thrust game of pretence. The winners are

57

the masks and poses which keep any nascent affection, desire or love firmly battened down. When morning comes they part without anything having taken place between them. The script originally made them part forever, but in the final version Pelagia returns to Bazyli. A triumph for genuine feeling, or a new gambit in the same game? Whichever it may be, the film was meant to be a defence of honesty, spontaneity and authenticism and an attack on sham, humbug and camouflage.

Innocent Sorcerers was a picture which should have made a big impact, since the Polish cinema had been accused, with some justice, of being so absorbed by the War that it had failed to notice there was such a thing as normal, everyday life in the country. But even from the point of view of Wajda's own *oeuvre* it was highly noteworthy: in both theme and style he was breaking new ground, and doing so, I imagine, from a deep-felt need to recharge his batteries and measure himself against the challenge of something never tried before. Wajda has told interviewers that he always

Tadeusz Łomnicki with Jerzy Skolimowski as the aggressive young boxer

dreamed of making a comedy (that had to wait until 1969—*Hunting Flies*) and that he wanted to replenish his stock-in-trade. Up to 1960 he had been exercising the same muscles first flexed in *A Generation*. To feel five years and four films later the urge for a change of pace seems very much to his credit; and all the more so as the metamorphosis was successful. For the first time in one of his films there were no fateful choices in which individual and national destinies hung in the balance: the stakes in this game were merely the outcome of a single night, to which the attitude of each side was in any case very much take-it-or-leave-it, the only danger being made to look silly. With the mood so relaxed all trace of Wajda's old sonorousness, the intensity of imagery into which everything had to be compressed—the particular and the symbolic, beauty and ugliness, history and contemporary relevance—was pared away to a crisp core of precise construction, understatement, sure timing of performance and witty, intelligent dialogue; all in all, a lively duel of words, gestures and poses, or, in

The humiliation of Skolimowski's boxer

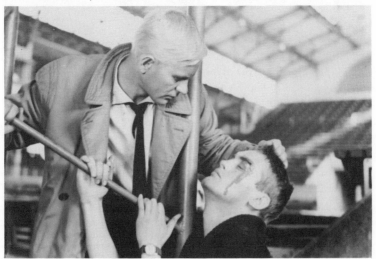

Krystyna Stypułkowska during the night-long strip game

Gombrowicz's phrase, grimaces. *Innocent Sorcerers* was also the first out-and-out actors' film made by Wajda: there was no spectacle, no evocative imagery, no pregnant scenery—just two players who had to carry the film by themselves. Since Polish cinema had always had more in common with Wajda's previous style than with this low-keyed approach, it should have been a fresh and rewarding experience.

The paradox is that almost everyone was disenchanted: the state producer, the critics (at any rate some of them) and Wajda himself. Had they all been carried away by a conviction that this was not what the "Wajda phenomenon" was about and that any attempt to re-model it or extend its range was bound to come to grief? Wajda himself noted on September 3, 1960, shortly after the film went on the floor: "I'm afraid nothing interesting can come out of this. What do I care about heroes of this sort! Are these supposed to be problems! They're not forced into anything!"[1] Here we can detect the apprehensions that must have come over him as soon as he found himself with a drama so much slighter than usual. Though he saw its point eventually, he was still plagued by the thought that he had got off on the wrong foot. In an interview eight years later he told me with distinct exasperation: "This film has flaws. Perhaps I shouldn't have gone along with the script as written, fascinatingly written, with the sparkle of the banter between the man and the girl. I should have looked for answers to the underlying question: how is it that there is a separate youth society and what are its idols? I know that they're not the American ones, that they spring from a small country and belong to a small group of youth, but it's equally obvious that there are wider phenomena behind this . . . With the benefit of hindsight I can now see that I bumped into someone then who was just what I needed and who was even there in the film: Skolimowski. He's the one it should have been about, not some fictional character. Only at the time he was just some obscure poet and Andrzejewski's assistant on the script."[2] Elsewhere he has frankly stated that Bazyli was a muddled character and his behaviour illogical. Why had not he and Pelagia ended up making love after all? What made them so impotent? Only the lack of authenticity? Or were there other barriers? Wajda feels these points should have been made explicit.

As for the critics, or a section of them, their complaints centred on the film's social implications. Here at last was the "contemporary subject" they had been clamouring for, but it was not what they had expected. In "Trybuna ludu," Janusz Wilhelmi, a literary critic, grasped the point *Innocent Sorcerers* was trying to make: "Don't be afraid of your longings and feelings! Shed your poses, be yourselves! As a general precept, this is no doubt an admirable moral and delivered in the best of faith. But does it solve the problem?" And he went on: "Shed your poses, be yourselves! Fair enough—but who is that? *Innocent Sorcerers* clearly implies that there are treasures of humanity buried under that crust of pose . . . But that just is not true. Dig down and you will find only the most limited of creatures lacking real human passions and real human interests. And, above all, extremely murky."[3] In "Zycie Warszawy," Poland's other major national daily, Stanisław Grzelecki wrote: "These young people are glorified adolescents. They may be sorcerers, but only in the sense of trying to bemuse us with their philosophy, whose chief tenet is 'what a bloody awful world.' They are not to be taken seriously."[4]

The charges in this indictment can be summed up as follows: Wajda chose as heroes characters who do not deserve to be elevated into subjects of art, and who have little to commend them from the social point of view; hence the influence of the film may prove dubious. Strange but harsh criticism! There was something disproportionate between so slight and downbeat a film, no more than an experiment in psychology and style, and the massive arguments rolled out against it taken from the arsenal of art with a crusading social purpose. It was like using a sledge-hammer to crack a nut: the film and the critics had their lines crossed.

On the other hand, one should remember that even then (not to mention today) Wajda's *oeuvre* had been placed on a plane where art invites judgement by the highest standards. It was Wajda who had taught the critics to expect significance from him, and not vice versa. He has never been a story-teller pure and simple, given to indulging in stylistic fireworks or aesthetic perfectionism. He is a film-maker for whom the purpose of telling a story has, in each and every one of his works, been to communicate something: his feelings, his reflections, his beliefs about people, the age, his nation.

If we look at *Innocent Sorcerers* from this angle we must conclude that for once the nuggets of truth he uncovered were a little disappointing. His younger fellow-directors—Polański, Skolimowski—have been more trenchant and incisive on the same subject.

Alina Janowska amid the bizarre surroundings of Serge Merlin's first refuge

8. New Lineaments of History—*Samson*

IN 1961 WAJDA RETURNED from contemporary waters to the setting of all his previous films—the War and the Occupation—and to the theme of suffering, despair and doom. The picture was *Samson*.

The "Samson" of the title is Jakub Gold (Serge Merlin) whose story begins before the War when as a freshman at Warsaw University he is set upon by a gang of anti-Semitic thugs, kills one of them in the ensuing brawl and is sentenced to a long term of imprisonment for manslaughter. In prison he meets a group of communists together with Pankrat, their ideological mentor. When the Germans invade Poland in 1939, the convicts are set at liberty, but shortly after the Polish defeat he finds himself in another form of incarceration—within the walls of the Warsaw Ghetto. Nothing daunted, he manages to escape and goes into hiding on the "Aryan" side, first in the bizarre household of a distant acquaintance (Alina Janowska) whose plight proves to be as desperate as his, and then with Malina (Jan Ciecierski), a man he had met in prison, and his daughter Kazia (Elżbieta Kępińska). He sits out the winter in their cellar, cut off from the world and the daylight, haunted by dread and despair. In a fit of panic after the death of Malina he rushes back to the Ghetto, to find that it has been razed to the ground. As he blunders through the streets of Warsaw with death lurking round every corner, he runs into another former fellow-prisoner and is taken to the hide-out of a secret communist organisation whose leader turns out to be Pankrat. Just as involvement in the Underground struggle is restoring his sense of purpose in life, disaster strikes: the Germans raid the premises and Gold is killed, but he dies fighting, and not in passive submission to the verdict of fate.

This story, with its distinct echoes of the biblical Samson, the giant laid low, was adapted from a novel by Kazimierz Brandys which formed part of a cycle about Poland in the Thirties and Forties. Written in the early Fifties, it had the Balzacian or Galsworthian structure of a rambling, far-flung chronicle travelling down the years through various spheres of society, with a set of recurring characters winding in and out of the texture. Brandys's aim was to record what he thought was the essence of the social, political, moral and psychological flux of the times and to reveal, emphasise or occasionally only illustrate their key socio-historical conditionings and necessities. Like most of the fiction written in those years, it presented the

THE CINEMA OF ANDRZEJ WAJDA

twists and turns of destiny as the result of social, class, political and ideological determinism, a point that was usually laboured: the very origin of a character—working class, capitalist, *lumpenproletariat*—more or less pre-determined his moral qualities and political allegiances. It was a formula which invited a certain, often simplistic "sociology" typical of the literature of the early Fifties. In this current Brandys kept afloat better than most by sheer literary skill and intellectual poise, qualities put to much better use later in such books as "Letters to Mme. Z." By the time the cinema reached *Samson* this type of literature was, however, in bad odour with the critics, a circumstance that was to affect the reception of the film.

Translating *Samson* to the screen proved difficult. For one reason, the aim was not simply to pictorialise this epic novel (or to illustrate a certain chunk of history), but to make the story of Jakub Gold epitomise the drama of a man at bay, which was the theme that interested Wajda: here the screenplay was a compromise. For another, Wajda saw the actual characterisation of Gold in rather different terms from the book, where he had been a giant who did not know his own strength: he wanted someone who would personify anxiety and anguish, and the casting of the young French actor Serge Merlin, slight of build, brooding, bewildered, went along these lines.

The most important thing omitted from Brandys's novel, however, was a view of history new to Wajda and one which coloured the whole treatment of human destiny. In his classic films—*Kanal* and *Ashes and Diamonds*—history was, as I have tried to show, seen as a blind, anonymous force smashing its way through life and leaving behind a trail of misery, pain and death. Wajda observed and registered the havoc but could not, or would not, look deeper into the machinery which caused it. It was only in *Samson* that, taking his cue from Brandys, he imposed some kind of logic and pattern on history and indicated its social, political and ideological mainsprings. Gold's fate is as tragic and inevitable as that of any of Wajda's other heroes; what is different is that the workings behind it are revealed, for the first time there is an intimation of the political, moral and class agencies responsible for his misfortunes. The sole opposition, not just to fascism, but to the terror and apathy of its victims, comes chiefly from the communists whom Gold first meets in prison and who later come to his rescue, rekindling his will to live and resist. It is worth noting, therefore, that we have not only a flat description of people who suffer and people who fight, but also an analysis of the forces which inflict these sufferings, of the people who bear guilt and responsibility.

This point was neatly grasped by Barthélemy Amengual in his study of Wajda, "En proie à l'histoire": "In *A Generation* and in *Kanał,* Wajda absolves his characters, while indicating their guilt: 'my heroes are not responsible.' In *Ashes and Diamonds* and *Lotna* the acquittal is total: it is History which is guilty. But beginning with *Samson* Wajda embarks on a re-appraisal of the very idea of responsibility . . . He then stumbles upon the Sartrian proposition of 'on ne fait pas ce qu'on veut et cependant on est responsable de ce qu'on est.' "[1] True enough: this new approach to the conformation of human destiny implies a new concept of responsibility— for oneself and for the world. In *Kanał* and *Ashes and Diamonds,* man pulverised by the juggernaut of history was seen only as an object, not as a subject; hence his passivity, his fatalistic acceptance of what is in any case inevitable. But once the mechanism of history has been laid bare and its undercurrents brought to light, man assumes a responsibility for himself, for his fellows and for his fate. The appearance of such a point of view in *Samson* should be regarded, therefore, as a new departure in the moral and philosophical content of Wajda's cinema, the elimination of a certain weakness or (as some critics had it) helplessness in its underpinning.

Wajda seemed at last to have found a way of penetrating the inscrutable figure of History which had featured so prominently in his films. The trouble was that his methods lacked the necessary touch of subtlety: he took from the novel, and in the process no doubt heightened, certain sociological and political axioms which, if not necessarily arbitrary, were made to seem so by the lack of circumstantiation in the plot and a certain tendency to iron out any motivation other than the social. At the same time the characters were modelled too simplistically on their social archetypes and so gave the impression of being little more than conventional cut-outs.

As a result, it is where the film aims at an epic structure, in its marking of the passage of time and its adumbration of the theme of social, political and historical determinism (and this was where the adaptation made heavy weather), that it was at its most faltering and unconvincing. The opening scenes—university, the anti-semitic fracas, the killing, the prison—look like potted information, and certainly not the episodes in a man's life, the prelude to his drama, that they are meant to be.

Paradoxically enough, *Samson* only begins to come to life and achieve a certain stature when Wajda seems to forget about that top-dressing of social and political determinism and switches from a description of the external world with its complex structures to an inspection of the inner world of Jakub Gold. These passages are powerful and of a piece, and thread into the film's capsulated history its real themes, ones which were not new to Wajda: the separation which leads to beleaguerment, the sense of peril which slowly paralyses the reflexes, the will, and the desire to live. Wajda's concern with the tragic nature of human destiny, with the straits into which it is driven, is given a new dimension: the hero is not a man who goes through all the motions of defence even though he knows they are futile, but one who is past any such gestures, who is resigned to dying. As played by Serge Merlin, Gold has the air of an alienated, lost creature in whom life is slowly running out. It is in these regions that the most moving sequences of *Samson* lie, and it seems certain that Wajda wanted the whole film to have such a flavour; he has since described it as a picture about isolation, "otherness," a dying fall, and not the social and political tap-roots of Nazism.

Critical judgements on *Samson* were divided, but mainly hostile. The chief complaints were not, for once, levelled at its aesthetics (mannered, baroque, and so on), nor even at its mood of gloom and despair. The principle charge was inaccuracy. One of the best Polish literary critics, Andrzej Kijowski, published a squib entitled "Anti-Wajda," which flailed its picture of the Occupation as completely garbled. "Enough of this rubbish!" he fulminated.[2] "Kijowski's whole article," wrote Konrad Eberhardt in an ironical rejoinder, "stems from a shattering discovery: the Occupation as presented by Wajda does not tally with the image preserved by the critic, his friends and the works of literature he admires . . . The vicissitudes of Jakub Gold must automatically, therefore, be a string of absurdities. Why did he kill the student (he could have injured him)? Why did he go to prison (he could have been given a suspended sentence)? Why did he help the man in the cemetery to escape (he could have stood by)? Why did he land up in the home of a Jewish woman with complexes (she could have been free of them)? In fact, he need not have even been a Jew, but a man called Kowalski and worked in a post-office. He needn't have lived in the first place."[3] But Wajda's inaccuracy was harped on: the prewar episode (the killing of the student on the university campus) was said to ring false and be historically unfounded; the situation in the Ghetto to be spuriously presented; the desperate flight back to the Ghetto when Gold is *in extremis* to be preposterous; even the home, complete with fountain, of the Jewish woman where he is first sheltered to be unheard of in Warsaw.

Such charges at first sound ludicrous and would suggest a state of

Opposite: Samson's symbolic emasculation by Kazia (Elżbieta Kępińska)

The ever-present mark of Judaism

muddle-headedness among the critics apparently blind to the distinction between fact and fiction. I suspect, however, that what they were really protesting at was something else, that what in fact they found so hard to swallow was the picture of a world made to measure and cut away to demonstrate its political, ideological, social and historical components. All this was present in the novel and it showed in certain parts of the film. It was in fact the over-simplified view of realities favoured by the literature and cinema of the Fifties, whose flaws had in the meantime been exposed and witheringly derided. Perhaps too witheringly: for, looking back, one can see that the Polish films of this period, even ones of the highest purpose, hardly ever tried to sketch in the world's social contours and preferred to cling to the concept of history as an overpowering, mysterious force.

Even Wajda himself, however, realised which parts of *Samson* were marred by lapses and *naïveté,* and which had the bite of human truth, since he has insisted that "the Occupation in *Samson* is only a backdrop and the Germans faceless. It is not the Occupation which matters, but the predicament of a hounded man."[4] One criticism must have rankled particularly, since it was the last he could have expected: that the drama of Jakub Gold is too abstract and divorced from its historical context. A curious accusation, when it was in *Samson* of all films that he had for the first time tried to place his cornered hero in the socio-political context of his times.

9. In Quest of Perfection—*Siberian Lady Macbeth*

A SCREEN VERSION of Nikolay Leskov's "Lady Macbeth of Mtsensk" had already been contemplated by Wajda before *Samson;* there was even the draft of a script which he had shown around, though without arousing any real interest in Poland. Doubtless the idea of a film-maker so completely immersed in Polish themes wishing to shoot a story with Shakespearean echoes laid in a Nineteenth-century Russian village seemed whimsical to say the least.

After the rough passage given to *Samson* in Poland, he took the project to Yugoslavia and made it for Avala Film in Belgrade. *Siberian Lady Macbeth (Sibirska Ledi Magbet)* was not a co-production, nor were there any other Poles involved (though the credits of all the films he subsequently directed abroad are thick with the names of Polish friends). It was a purely Yugoslav picture, the co-writer being Sveta Lukić, the director of photography Alexandar Sekulović, and the leads played by the well-known Yugoslav actors, Olivera Marković, Ljuba Tadić and Bojan Stupica.

Wajda's first non-Polish film was also the first which had nothing to do with the destinies or dilemmas of his countrymen. Furthermore, there are few antecedents for outsize heroines like Leskov's in the tradition of Polish art with which Wajda has always identified so closely. The point once came up in a conversation that psychological introspection is more or less alien to Polish literature, which has always preferred to confront man with the community and history rather than with his own self, with his passions, or with other men individually. Wajda eagerly concurred: "Yes, that's our literature exactly. It comes out best in its women, or rather their conspicuous absence! Can you imagine any greater freak than literature without women? It's proof that it was never introspective, never 'psychological' . . ."[1] What then was Wajda of all people, a film-maker more deeply implanted in the Polish literary tradition than any other, thinking of in deciding to film the portrait of a *femme fatale* written by a Nineteenth-century Russian writer? Does *Siberian Lady Macbeth* have none of the features of his previous work?

The setting is a forlorn Russian village in which is the house of Izmaylov, a local merchant, a large prosperous establishment with yards and outbuildings forming a form of insulated stockade. Here lives Katerina Lvovna

(Olivera Marković), the daughter-in-law of Boris Izmaylov (Bojan Stupica), the real master of the household, whose young son Zinovi is far away travelling on business. Katerina is bored and drifts restlessly around the house; it does not seem, however, to be the absence of her husband which has set her on edge, since we know their marriage is not a happy one, both pining over the lack of children. There appears an earthy, rakish swineherd, Sergey (Ljuba Tadić), who at once senses Katerina's despondency and tenseness and quickly becomes her lover. As soon as the conquest has been made, however, he comes under her thumb. When Boris finds out that his son is being cuckolded, he has Sergey flogged to within an inch of death. In her fury Katerina takes a calculated revenge by putting rat poison in the mushrooms which her father-in-law is continually and neurotically wolfing, and he dies in convulsions. There now begins an idyllic interlude: Sergey's scars heal, and lust mellows into love, but by this time the whole village knows of the affair. Her husband comes home unexpectedly and guesses what is going on, but Katerina has a special brand of pride which will not allow her to release Sergey. Zinovi is murdered and Sergey buries his corpse in the pigsty. The lovers are now left by themselves—and seemingly in the clear—until a distant cousin arrives with her small son. By law the boy is the heir to the Izmaylov property, and a new contest begins: over the inheritance, over the threat to her love for Sergey, and over her own dignity. The cousin is arrogant and bent on humiliating Katerina. During a religious procession, when the house is empty, Katerina and Sergey try to suffocate the boy, but are noticed by the crowd which bursts into the house and takes them away. Sentenced to banishment for life, they set off on a nightmarish march to Siberia, resembling a column of concentration camp deportees. Sergey's eye soon strays to a young fellow-prisoner, Sonya, and his manner towards the woman whose love drove her to murder becomes increasingly truculent and insulting. While they are crossing the Volga, Katerina, frenzied with rage, pushes Sonya off the raft and jumps in after her to drown amid the ice-floes and mists of the river.

Siberian Lady Macbeth is the story of a woman of uncommonly headstrong and commanding character whose drive and wilfulness make her tower over her environment. Everyone around her is squalid and puny, even her lover—a feckless, weak-kneed good-for-nothing content to be her creature for as long as she is in control, but unfaithful the moment she is manacled. They are not partners in life and crime: one is an individual of domineering stature, the other a stooge.

Olivera Marković

The Leskov story was meant as a Russian paraphrase of the Shakespeare tragedy, and the motivation in Wajda's film underwent further shifts. Ambition and the lust for power are there, but only in the background, eclipsed by the irrepressible, unbridled passion of a woman whose hidden fires are suddenly revealed. There is a certain biological plausibility in this: Katerina cannot have children by her husband, and this failure has increased her frustration and scorn for her environment. The driving force, however, is an irrational, insatiable, desperate love of the kind described by the great Romantic writers of the Nineteenth century, a naked, elemental force ploughing through life. This idea of love as a destroyer is new to Wajda: both in *Ashes and Diamonds* and *A Generation* love regenerated human nature and sublimated the hero.

Some thought at the time that Wajda had gone off at a tangent to his real concerns, but if we remember that "Macbeth" is one of his favourite plays (he directed a TV production in 1969), it is clear that he must have found some quality in the story which arrested him. The fact is that an artist of Wajda's stamp is bound to be attracted to people beyond the norm, who may be saints or sinners, but are magnificent in their virtue or wickedness. "I am only interested in characters on the grand scale, confronted by

71

the fundamental alternatives of existence. They are the only ones who can die on a rubbish heap, who can take part in a cavalry charge against tanks, who can trudge through stinking sewers . . . I am interested in someone who is in opposition to great ideals or who accepts them, but not in someone who trots along in the footsteps of others."[2]

Katerina Lvovna is one of these characters "on a grand scale" who people Wajda's imagination. Violent and possessive, protective and domineering in her attitude to men, she re-appears, caricatured, seven years later in his satirical comedy *Hunting Flies,* a venomous dig at the matriarchical threat to contemporary civilisation. Although this is a marginal theme in Wajda's cinema, it is a recurrent one; *Siberian Lady Macbeth* is neither its first nor its last outing.

The drama unfolds within the enclosed space of the Izmaylov household, moving back and forth between bed-chamber, living room and courtyard: it moves outside these confines only rarely and incidentally. The direction is so consistent and emphatic in this aspect that we might almost be watching

The period atmosphere of SIBERIAN LADY MACBETH

a play rather than a film. The scenery, too, resembles a theatre set: skeletal, significant, distributed strictly according to the requirement of the "business"—here the long table of the feast which ends in a moment of sudden panic, there the window, which is not just part of a room, but the means of Sergey's furtive entrances and exits from Katerina's bed. None of the furnishings, fittings and props have a "natural presence"; they are there only if they are stageworthy. The same purpose is served by the profusion of Russian exotica over which the camera lingers pointedly: a log cabin, Katerina's pigtails, the men's beards, icons, samovars, the onion domes of the church which is continually sighted in the background. The point of all this was clearly grasped by René Prédal in his essay on the film: "Wajda concentrates the action in a few places . . . and opens out the drama as little as possible: exteriors are rare and have about them something of a paroxysm."[3]

Perhaps the most striking thing is that the whole story of *Siberian Lady Macbeth* is staged according to the classic rules of drama. At the very beginning of the film, barely has Katerina been presented and her early mood of fretfulness established than there ensues a conversation with her father-in-law which serves as a model exposition, informing us of the *dramatis personae,* the atmosphere, and the conflict generated by her childlessness. From there on the film develops with a logic worthy of time-honoured theatrical canons: the poison first appears in the hand of old Boris, and we later see him voraciously guzzling his beloved mushrooms, into a plate of which it has been sprinkled when the first crisis comes; and so on. The reason I dwell on this precision is that it creates a system of psychological and circumstantial compulsions which lead as inexorably to murder as in the original "Macbeth." Once committed, Katerina and the acquiescent Sergey *could not* do other than they did. The plunge into crime is gradual, but psychologically totally convincing. It does not end, as in "Macbeth," in madness, but it has the same cast-iron inevitability. This presumably is what led René Prédal to conclude: "Wajda a donc effectué une véritable lecture shakespearienne de l'oeuvre de Leskov."[4]

We can see, therefore, that in this film Wajda attained a certain dramatic discipline, a certain perfectionism of psychological analysis, and a certain functional style of *mise-en-scène.* In spite, or perhaps precisely because, of this the film remains an effective, but chilly picture, the kind one can admire but not enthuse over. Nowhere did it strike the sparks of emotion which *A Generation* or *Ashes and Diamonds* generated.

Especially in Poland. *Siberian Lady Macbeth* was released in 1962, almost a year after its Yugoslav *première;* it did badly at the box-office and little better at the hands of the critics. Attention was drawn to the difference between this film and everything that Wajda had made before, but this was tempered by the appearance of the word "academicism." At all events *Siberian Lady Macbeth* afforded negative proof that the excitement generated by his earlier (and subsequent) works came not from their aesthetic accomplishment but from their tingling and irresistible emotional, social and political immediacy.

The "nightmarish" journey to Siberia

10. Encore the Next Generation—*Love at Twenty*

IN 1961 a French producer, Pierre Roustang, hit on the idea of a portmanteau film set in various countries and made by various directors. The linking theme was to be the generation of twenty-year-olds or, in his grandiose phrase, "the inscrutable youth of the atomic age and technological civilisation." It was thought that the young film-makers who were coming on the scene would be the very people to illuminate the patterns of behaviour, thought and love among this new breed of youth, a subject that was eventually run into the ground, but which in the early Sixties was still something of a fresh field. *Love at Twenty* (*L'amour à vingt ans*) had episodes from France (directed by François Truffaut), Italy (Renzo Rossellini), West Germany (Marcel Ophüls) and Japan (Shintaro Ishihara). Roustang also wanted a Polish story and approached Wajda and screenwriter Jerzy Stawiński, both of whom were regarded as representatives of the "young" Polish cinema which had made a certain *éclat* during the late Fifties.

Their earlier films, however, had been soundings of a different and older generation which by this time was well into its thirties; between them and the twenty-year-olds there stood something of a wall. Nevertheless the Poles accepted the invitation: Wajda was not, after all, uninterested in this "next" generation—had he not already tried in *Innocent Sorcerers* to plumb its "inscrutability"? Another point was that that film had left something of a bitter taste, not only because of the rebukes it had earned from some Polish critics, but principally because he himself was far from happy with its artistic shape. His doubts seem to have sprung from the film's overly-detached inspection of its subject. "Apart from one or two scenes," he has said, "*Innocent Sorcerers* is a film I don't like very much . . . Its trouble is the absence of a point of view, of my own attitude to these young people."[1] What were his feelings about this "inscrutable" generation? Benevolent or frosty? *Love at Twenty* provided an opportunity to make his position clear.

A seasoned screenwriter, Stawiński drafted a number of treatments of the suggested theme. But one point on which he and Wajda seem to have made up their minds from the start was that instead of trying to see things

from the twenty-year-olds' point of view (as Truffaut did in his contribution), they would do better to reverse the angle and look from the perspective of the generation to which they themselves belonged and whose biography they had charted in their films. "When I was asked to sound off about 'love at twenty,'" Wajda has recalled, "I realised it was beyond me, since I belong to a generation which is unmistakably older, which has the War and the Resistance in its system, whereas the youth of today are divided into two groups: those who remember the War and those who don't. So it struck me that the thing to do was to point to the conflict between these two generations, to the impossibility of deep and lasting communication between them."[2]

Paradoxically, therefore, though quite in accordance with the logic of Wajda's and Stawiński's work, their story became less of a study of the up-and-coming generation than a valediction to the one on the way out, run-down, stale and emasculated by a hum-drum existence, with a streak of heroism still lingering, but fast fading into figures of fun. The following is the basic plot to the Polish episode in *Love at Twenty*.

In the Warsaw zoo a child has fallen into the polar bear pit. As the bystanders look on in frozen horror, apart from a youth hurriedly trying to snap so dramatic a scene, a drab, slightly podgy man in wire-rimmed spectacles (Zbigniew Cybulski) pushes forward, climbs coolly and unhesitatingly over the barrier, retrieves the child, walks off, finds he has lost his fountain pen, turns back and toys with the idea of going back into the pit to recover it. We have now been presented with all the *dramatis personae:* on the one hand, the twenty-year-olds who have been watching the whole incident, on the other, the middle-aged rescuer about whom we as yet know nothing. Intrigued, a young girl (Barbara [Kwiatkowska-] Lass) gets talking with him and invites him home where she is throwing a party: a painful contrast emerges between her flushed, callowly insensitive friends and the "polar bear man," now a meter inspector collecting bills door to door, but once a resistance hero (who may have marched through the sewers or taken part in the events of *A Generation*) pathetically regaling the company with what seem to them tall stories about this stirring past, an obvious has-been, but with an element of stature. As he shuffles away in the early hours much the worse for drink, he is sent off with a harmless, though in the circumstances mocking, nursery song about a "sleepy old bear."

It is a simple story simply told, without any of the symbolism and ornate

Opposite: Wajda and Cybulski during the filming of LOVE AT TWENTY

visual effects which feature so prominently in most of Wajda's films. Perhaps the knowledge that he was making a picture which, though concerned with things Polish, was basically addressed to a non-Polish audience, stayed his hand from any more esoteric allusions, metaphors and associations (and yet, as in *Ashes and Diamonds*, as in *The Wedding* in 1972, he could not resist ending the film with a stupefied dance to the rhythm of the same ironic tune used as the setting of Wyspiański's famous lines about the yokel and his lost golden horn). Be that as it may, the film has a simplicity, freshness and spontaneity after which the Polish critics, always attacking the "baroque" Wajda, had hankered. It was even seen as a turning point: Aleksander Jackiewicz, who regularly took him to task for his stiltedness and poker-work, was led by this very quality of understatement to hail it as a near-masterpiece.[3] Few could have suspected that shortly afterwards, in *Ashes,* there would be an abrupt swing back to the orotund and opera-like strain in Wajda's cinema.

For Wajda himself this modest little film seems to possess considerable significance. It rounds off a certain cycle in his *oeuvre,* setting the seal on the biography of a generation which he and the other film-makers of the "Polish school," as well as Zbigniew Cybulski, had created. Its heroes are running to seed, work for the electricity board, and reminisce about the years of struggle only when they are drunk. This is all that is left of those magnificent young men with blazing eyes and grim features. A harsher conclusion was reached only by Tadeusz Konwicki (a fascinating writer, but as a film-maker woefully underrated outside Poland) a few years later in *Salto,* where he showed the same "veteran," again played by Zbigniew Cybulski, but now a paranoiac impostor, a fake who has lost all identity, in whom truth and sham, memories and the present, authenticity and histrionics, have become twisted into an agonising Gordian knot. Had Polish cinema reached a point where it was beginning to mock its own idols? No: for Wajda it was merely a moment to take stock of these heroes and rediscover in them, despite their grotesque and bumbling air, a certain grandeur—particularly in contrast to the next generation.

As seen by Wajda, it is singularly vapid, frivolous, self-absorbed and spineless. Not by any means an alluring picture: when the accident with the child takes place, the reaction of one of the young men is symptomatic—he takes out his camera; when the meter inspector launches forth on his reminiscences at the party, they are shrugged off as mere drunken meanderings. The young feel no longing for brave actions, no envy of their elders' experience which they so painfully lack. It was only a few years later that

Jerzy Skolimowski, the true biographer of this generation, showed in *Barrier* that beneath the pose of indifference and egoism there did in fact lurk some kind of craving for deeds out of the ordinary. When Skolimowski's young protagonist comes out into the street after a meeting with "veterans," he too feels the need to fight some battle, but the only thing in sight is a car. The bizarre duel that follows can be read as an admission of this simmering hunger for heroic challenges in an age of "petty stabilisation"—as it is called in Poland.

Wajda's verdict on youth is, therefore, unqualified, outspoken and flinty, without a hint of sympathy or admiration. "I got this matter off my chest," he has said, "in *Love at Twenty*. I spoke my mind there about this youth whom I neither understand nor like. I am not on their side."[4] In the end he did what he appears to have wanted, but failed, to do in *Innocent Sorcerers*. There, out of fidelity to the screenplay, he had reserved judgement and contented himself with scrutiny of some of the psychological characteristics of "inscrutable youth." In *Love at Twenty* he fired a broadside, direct and point-blank.

And yet, for all its withering criticism, there is a note of acceptance in the film. The clock cannot be stopped, and there is no call for putting weary heroes-turned-clerks on pedestals. Life must be taken as it comes, even though the succeeding generations it brings are not to our liking. This point was made more emphatically six years later in *Everything for Sale,* where Wajda observed the desperate exertions of Daniel, the young actor, to step into the shoes of a missing friend and predecessor. This, he says even more forthrightly, is a painful process, but one there is no avoiding, any more than the youngster's gibes at the "sleepy old bear," as he lurches away from his meeting with people who understand nothing but have the edge over him of youth.

11. Not Only History at Issue—*Ashes*

WORK BEGAN on *Ashes* (*Popioły*) in the early spring of 1964 and ended in the autumn of 1965. Prior to its *première* at the end of September 1965 some facts and figures were published: the film had taken 666 days to make, of which 304 had been spent before the cameras; the locations were shot in Poland and Bulgaria; in one of the battle scenes (Raszyn) 1,300 persons had taken part and, all told, several thousand extras, 116 professional actors and eleven historical advisers had been engaged; the props ran to 1,700 uniforms, 900 muskets (only 200 in working order), 100 thoroughbreds, a pack of specially-trained wolves, and so on. The reason for quoting these statistics is not to impress or repel readers with the sheer size of *Ashes,* but only to indicate how utterly different it was from anything Wajda had done before. All his previous pictures, even *Lotna* with its fair share of sweep and movement, were basically low-keyed affairs without large sets and milling crowds, without, in fact, those 1,300 guns. For Wajda *Ashes* was a new venture and very much of a gamble.

During the shooting, his assistant and friend, Andrzej Żuławski (now a director in his own right *The Third Part of the Night* (*Trzecia część nocy*) and *The Devil* (*Diabeł*)) published a regular progress report in the weekly "Film" under the heading "A Diary of *Ashes.*" In one of the early entries he mused over the sort of work it was going to be: "A film about a strange snowbound land . . . where carriages flounder in the mud only a stone's throw from the Royal Castle in Warsaw? A film about the mirage of liberty and reform which led this country to march behind Napoléon and leave thousands of dead behind in Italy, San Domingo, Spain? A film about three heroes, of whom one is brain, the second heart, and the third instinct? Is this filmable? And even if it is, how to avoid being submerged by the extras, the pyrotechnics, the cavalry, the regalia of uniform? This is Wajda's great headache, all the worse since our cinema's experience of battle scenes amounts to not much more than one Grünwald."[1] Nevertheless, a few weeks later he was noting that "Wajda, who has not made a film in Poland since *Love at Twenty,* has come to life and blossomed on the set."[2]

A more awkward problem, however, than surmounting the mechanics of

Opposite: a statuesque Beata Tyszkiewicz in ASHES

Aristocratic poise: Beata Tyszkiewicz and Daniel Olbrychski

the production was the actual adaptation of *Ashes,* a sprawling, quintessentially Polish and—to foreigners—baffling book which has become a classic. It is not a straightforward historical novel in the Dumas *genre,* but a giant historical and historio-philosophical fresco which resembles, if anything, Stendhal or Tolstoy. Its author, Stefan Żeromski (1864–1925), regarded as one of the greatest modern Polish writers, was an heir to the stirring Romantic tradition of Nineteenth-century Polish literature, while at the same time remaining thoroughly immersed in the concerns of his own day. *Ashes* was written in 1904, and was a panoramic, multi-storeyed account of the times a century earlier when the Poles, following the partitioning of their country by Russia, Austria and Prussia and the failure of the Kościuszko Insurrection, threw in their lot with Napoléon in whom they saw a liberator of Europe and Poland, and at all events their enemies' enemy.

The plot of *Ashes* follows the campaigns of the Polish legions which fought with Napoléon against the Prussians and Austrians, then touches on the ephemeral Duchy of Warsaw which was set up by Napoléon (and fell with him), describes the fighting in Spain and on San Domingo, and ends with Napoléon setting off on the march to Moscow. Żeromski was dealing, therefore, with a period of crucial importance in Polish history, considered the seedbed of the processes which determined the behaviour and nature of the Poles throughout the Nineteenth century and well into the Twentieth. In the twists and turns of this complex story, spanning many years and many countries, set in times of war and times of peace, amid endless wanderings, encounters and partings, tempestuous loves, friendships and hates, there was fused a synthesis of what came to be called "Polishness."

The novel was written at the turn of the century, and its style and

Filming the sleigh ride (Olbrychski on horse;
Wajda in foreground beside camera)

climate bear the stamp of this period. As in Germany and Scandinavia, this era marked a return to Romantic themes and a tumescent, over-wrought turn of phrase. Associated with a movement known as "Young Poland," Żeromski's writing was feverish to the point of hysteria and pitched in a key of emotional *afflatus* which never flagged. The turgid prose of his novels tends to daunt the contemporary reader, but there are nuggets of genuine gold which can reward patience. More on account of his imitators than himself there was even coined the term "Żeromski-ese," of which Wiktor Woroszylski wrote, in an enthusiastic review of the film, that "it has been identified in the reader's mind with an impractical, naive idealism, essentially spurious and embarrassing. And then there is the language, swollen by hyperbole, thick with purple patches, and, especially in the lyrical and love scenes, intolerably gamey."[3]

The novel had all the ingredients calculated to appeal to Wajda: the theme of "Polishness," the fluctuating fortunes of its principals, that incredibly impassioned atmosphere—and an abundance of ready-made spectacle into the bargain. Here also lay the source of the difficulties in adapting this sprawling epic, which could easily swamp the film-maker with its over-abundance of riches. Wajda and his screenwriter, Aleksander Ścibor-Rylski, himself a film director as well as novelist, decided, instead of merely picking out one strand, to try and accommodate everything they conceivably could and remain as faithful to Żeromski as possible. Most of the moments of both inspiration and bathos in the film are attributable to this fidelity. How extreme it was can be seen from an episode recorded by Andrzej Żuławski: "One thing that seemed totally baffling was what to do with the business of the Wandering Soldier who shuffles in, sits down and for the next forty pages holds forth about the tragic story of the Legions . . . From the outset everyone agreed that having an actor shuffle in, sit down and hold forth was out of the question since the audience would be sent straight to sleep. So he was turned into an emblematic figure who enters with the words 'Long live the Emperor' and shows his Napoleonic uniform. That was how we shot it, but when we saw the rushes, it proved to be even more deadly. Towards the end of the filming, when the style of Żeromski's language was beginning to ooze out of every pore in the screen, Wajda decided to do the Soldier's tale as written: so he shuffles in, sits down and holds forth."[4]

The film, which begins with the bald credit "Stefan Żeromski: Ashes" (a deliberate stressing of its fidelity to the original), is divided into "chapters," each of which has a caption taken from the novel. There are twenty-four of these, and the film runs for roughly four hours, though

A first glimpse of the Polish legions in Spain

Wajda had originally believed he could tell the story in not much over two. In the first part—twelve chapters—almost all the key characters make their appearance, though the dominant figure is Rafał Olbromski, the son of a backwoods landowner, impulsive, headstrong, eager to soak up life, but still an impressionable rough diamond (this was the screen *début* of Daniel Olbrychski who became, after this film, Wajda's favourite actor next to Cybulski, and acquired a popularity to match). To make his way in the world he leaves his father's estate to go to Warsaw where he becomes the secretary of the saturnine Prince Gintułt (Piotr Wysocki) whom he comes to admire and hate. He joins the Freemasons, tries to woo the statuesque Elżbieta (Beata Tyszkiewicz) and falls in love with the wife of the Master of the Lodge, Helena de With (Pola Raksa). At every step of the story, in the conversations, the reminiscences, or merely in the background, there

Two combat scenes from ASHES involving the Polish legions

French troops advance (above) and vigorous hand-to-hand fighting

continually hovers the question of Poland, anxiety over her future, talk about taking up arms, anticipation of liberty being recovered. In the second half the burden of the action shifts to Olbromski's friends, Krzysztof Cedro (Bogusław Kierc), a young, extremely delicate aristocrat, as sensitive as some exotic plant and still unblooded. The film now follows the dramatic stages of his initiation into manhood. Together with Olbromski he flees from occupied Poland and enrolls in the Polish Legions in Spain, where he takes part in the capture of Saragossa and the legendary charge of the Polish cavalry at Samosierra. In the course of events he suffers agonies of doubt, for it is a paradox of history (one which both the novel and the film especially emphasise) that the Poles fighting for the liberty of their own nation were simultaneously engaged in crushing Spain's. "I did not join the army," says Cedro's friend, Captain Wyganowski, "to burn Spanish peasants alive." Then follows the return to Poland, the Duchy of Warsaw, the Battles of Raszyn and Sandomierz, and a re-encounter with Olbromski. The story ends with the Poles marching off on Napoléon's Russian campaign. The final chapter of the film, captioned "Word of Honour" ("Słowo honoru"), shows a snow-covered plain and Napoléon's retinue riding up from the distance; among them is Cedro, serving the Emperor to the bitter end. Meanwhile Olbromski is lurching over the same plain, blinded, frozen, wreathed in straw and dying; Napoléon's entourage pass him without a word.

All this is related in a fluctuating rhythm dictated by the structure of the "chapters"; some are staccato and dramatic, others leisurely and loose-knit, others still purely illustrative, informing the viewer of developments "elsewhere" and "in the meantime." The multiplicity and variety of time, place, character and action (from intimate *tête-à-têtes* to sweeping battles) make *Ashes* at times seem over-charged. "The aesthetics of excess" was how Barbara Mruklik in her Polish monograph on Wajda described the style of the film, and certainly one can feel a continual straining for the highest pitch of dramatic and visual intensity in every scene, in every shot, almost in every gesture. The result is a certain theatricality, a tendency to spot-light people, incidents, and even backgrounds, as though they were part of a pageant. It was this that led some people to wave the word "operatic" at *Ashes*. With it went Wajda's old habit of piling up abrupt contrasts: beauty set off by ugliness and gore, loftiness by crudity, and so on. Critics, especially in Poland, had always taxed him with a penchant for the baroque, and if ever there was a film of which this might have been true, it is *Ashes*.

Opposite: Daniel Olbrychski in the burning city of Saragossa

Żeromski seemed to have released in him all the predilections which in other circumstances, working with a different kind of literary raw material, had been kept under control.

The fact is that there is a certain parallel between Żeromski's prose and the visual style of Wajda's *Ashes*. "If we were to analyse," to quote Barbara Mruklik once again, "the argosy of devices in Żeromski's lexicon, we would have little trouble in detecting counterparts in the structure of the film. We would find a similar style of imagery deriving from the same processes of thought and response."[5] In this sense the blame for the aesthetic strictures levelled at the film (though they were not weighty) belongs as much to Żeromski as to Wajda. "Histrionics, excess, rhetoric," the critic Rafał Marszałek observed acutely, "appear wherever there is no line drawn between thought and feeling. It is one which is not always firmly etched either in Żeromski's novels or Wajda's films. His images are never ascetic, any more than Żeromski's contemplation of the world is cool and precisely organised. In their works we have over-coloured emotions, exalted gestures, passions caught on the boil . . . If *Ashes* draws our attention to the reefs in Wajda's *oeuvre,* we should also bear in mind the *difficult* greatness of Żeromski."[6]

The baroque flamboyance of the film spilled over into the run-up to its *première*. In the Mickiewicz Museum of Literature a large exhibition was put on of scenery, props and dummies from *Ashes;* it was designed with a typical feel for dramatic effects by none other than Wajda himself. The opening took place in Warsaw's largest theatre, the Congress Hall, and was preceded by a parade of extras in period costume, also staged by Wajda. At first the reviewers were enthusiastic to a man. Then they seemed to be struck by second thoughts.

To understand what brought about this metamorphosis a closer look needs to be taken not at the style but at the message embodied in the film. Adhering closely to the novel, Wajda had not confined himself simply to relating the adventures and adversities of his heroes. At the heart of his crowded tapestry there lay something more than individual vicissitudes: an account of the fortunes of a whole nation in the throes of reforging its identity, disowning its age-old feudal legacy, digesting the idea of the equality and brotherhood of all men and, above all, turning the recovery of liberty into the overriding emotional and intellectual concern of every Pole, of the whole culture and civilisation of his country. Wajda painted this huge collective portrait, warts and all. The Poles in his film are purblind as well as magnificent, petty-minded as well as heroic; the nation is held

*Rafał (Daniel Olbrychski), at right, is initiated into freemasonry
on the recommendation of Prince Gintułt (Piotr Wysocki), at left*

up as a creature to be both honoured and condemned. Throughout the film
there runs a strong streak of bitterness: the experiences of the Poles at the
beginning of the Nineteenth century form a chapter of glory, it is true,
but they are also a warning to contemporaries.

In all of this Wajda was echoing Żeromski, a point affirmed by two distinguished literary historians of the day. Professor Kazimierz Wyka wrote:
"The great heroine of the work is History, and so Wajda has produced a
vision of history and the human destinies involved, which is, like the original, passionate, bitter, tragic, and forbidding, and, like the original, un-
acceptable to the hagiographers. But that is the way Żeromski saw history,
not strutting and glamourised to gladden the heart, but weary and be-
draggled, with festering, unbandaged wounds, and moreover cruel and
squalid, betraying its professed aims, slipping out of the grip of those who

91

hope to carry it."[7] And Professor Stefan Żółkiewski added: "Wajda has not in any way impoverished the profundity and responsibility of Żeromski's historio-philosophy. More, he has updated and amplified his lovers' quarrel with the Polish national character."[8]

It was this "up-dating" which set off an explosion no one had foreseen. Except perhaps Wajda, who had said in an interview: "I am not interested in the literature of national consensus, in the literature of reconciliation all round. I am interested in Żeromski, who is full of bitterness, full of contradictions which are real contradictions. I mean to show them on the screen since I treat the public as adults who can make up their own minds. I am against creating a new mythology in place of the old one."[9]

The first to open fire was the critic and essayist, Krzysztof Teodor Toeplitz in an article pointedly headed "Historical Tragedy and Absurd

Napoléon (Janusz Zakrzeński) and his retinue at the close of ASHES

Tragedy." He maintained, citing Żeromski's own later interpretations, that the view of history in the novel did not by any manner of means suggest that the fortunes of Poland and the Poles were a string of tragic absurdities— as the film seemed to suggest.[10] At the same time the film was attacked by another literary historian, Professor Jan Zygmunt Jakubowski, and a writer, Zbigniew Załuski, who had already in a book published earlier, "The Seven Deadly Sins" ("Siedem grzechów głównych"), flayed all those (and there were many Polish films among his targets) who had harped on the theme of unnecessary, wasted heroism. He insisted that the numerous episodes in Polish history traditionally labelled "futile heroism" or even "folly" were in fact examples of calculated courage and foresight. (This pro-heroic slant was to find its way into the Polish cinema in the late Sixties and re- lease a spate of war films which had no room for any dilemmas, tragedies or disasters, but only pure heroism wreathed in the halo of victory.) Both these writers, echoed by many others, splashed their extremely critical opinions over the columns of the press, on the air, on television, etc. "Night- mare, cruelty, whimsicality," inveighed Professor Jakubowski, "these are the elements that have been focussed in the rich panorama of the Legions' annals. I am prepared to face up boldly to the history of the nation and take a critical view of the instances of backwardness, irresponsibility and class selfishness. But I shall not cast glib aspersions on those who for decades laid down their lives 'on the flat earth and at the bottom of the unfathom- able sea.' This is something that has not been understood or was beyond the grasp of the makers of the film who have usurped the title 'Ashes.' "[11] Zbigniew Załuski: " 'Ashes' is a searing and devastating book, the fiercest denunciation of atrocities committed by the writer's own nation to be found in world literature. It would be hard and, I would think, pointless to 'sharpen' Żeromski, to go one better than him in the harshness of his verdict. But Żeromski was entitled to pass judgement since, like an impartial court, he let both sides have their say and heard both prosecution and de- fence. The makers of the film have handed all the arguments, emotional as well as rational, to the prosecution . . . The defence has been refused a hearing."[12] The *coup de grâce* was delivered by Professor Jakubowski during a television discussion: "In the work of national education Żeromski is close to us; the film, on the other hand, is pernicious."[13]

The complaint was not so much that Wajda had garbled Żeromski, as that his portrait of the Poles was too blackly painted. The controversy became heated in the extreme. Newspapers began publishing letters from readers in the following vein: "Why has Wajda so manifestly failed to understand the profound and deeply patriotic content of 'Ashes'? What led him . . . to select fragments of the book and present them in a way that warps the author's intention?"[14] Another reader indignantly wrote in after a visit to the *Ashes* exhibition in the Mickiewicz Museum: "Are these soldiers? They are mercenaries, drunks and cut-throats . . . I have heard all about the need to 'take the lid off causes of ignominy, to oppose varnishing the truth, to bequeath lessons to posterity.' I cannot accept such explanations. As a historian I must protest and protest I do."[15] In a letter to another weekly Jan Wyka, a writer, stated: "In the contentious passions of a highly sheepish public opinion, the discussion has produced the conflicting historical definitions of those who are willing to let the truth be stained with blood and those who with the inspiration of faith shroud it in a spotless sheet. Even a faintly audible note of chauvinism has recovered its heroic ring. A dispute about the past? Surely it is also a dispute between the opposites of the present day, a dispute of dissensions and divisions?"[16]

Why was it that tempers were so ruffled? Were people really becoming agitated over some particular interpretation of history, over the question of whether the Poles of 150 years ago were paragons of virtue and wisdom, or frivolous, demented and bloodthirsty? The answer, of course, is that the issue was not one man's view of events in the past, but the moral he drew from it for the present generation. The controversy over Wajda's *Ashes* detonated a wider ideological and political discussion which ranged beyond the problems of literary adaptation or film in general. It polarised, on the one hand, those who through contemporary political logic demanded the upholding of a belief in the virtue, wisdom and maturity of the Polish people and those, on the other, who wanted to find, in a more national, incisive and argumentative look at the nation, bearings for contemporary behaviour. After the *première* of *Ashes* Wajda was fiercely attacked by the former and defended by the latter. This clash occurred once more in 1969, with the appearance of *Landscape after the Battle*.

12. 'Nothing Went Right'—*Gates to Paradise*

IN 1213, under the papacy of Innocent III, a shepherd boy in the south-east region of France heard a voice from heaven telling him that the time had come for the children to deliver the Holy Land from heathen rule. So began the bizarre episode of the Children's Crusade. A band of boys and girls between eight and sixteen years of age marched off in the grip of a powerful vision.

This historical event had long intrigued Wajda, who must have been very much alive to the uncanny and tragic implications of children obsessed by a belief that they could succeed where four massed crusades had failed, setting out in a trance for that legendary Jerusalem—which they never reach. A story with so much natural drama and tragedy must have seemed supremely filmable.

Wajda suggested the subject to Jerzy Andrzejewski, the author of *Ashes and Diamonds,* who kept procrastinating, unable to make up his mind about the form it could best take: short story, film script, epic novel? In the end it came out as a hundred-page novella (originally planned as the first chapter of a novel several times the length), a brilliant *tour de force* which described with dazzling precision a single night of this pilgrimage when the children make their Easter confession and unburden themselves of their anxieties, sins, and true intentions. Both here and in the screenplay, the emphasis was on the psychological, moral and philosophical currents of the story: impurity and sin, falsehood and truth, love and lust. Its outward contours—the mechanics of the expedition, its purpose, its tragedy—were only adumbrated in the background. They may however, have been the very things which Wajda most wanted to bring out.

The film was to be produced by Avala Film in Belgrade, and after various hitches it eventually went on the floor in 1966. Wajda arrived in Yugoslavia with a fairly definite picture of what he meant to do. On this point his "Exegesis to *Gates to Paradise*" is revealing: it blocks out answers to all the problems of style and content posed by the given conditions. For instance, the film was to be shot entirely on location, in scenery resembling the south of France. Could such an intimate drama stand up to the wide open spaces of such exteriors? In his "Exegesis" Wajda wrote: "Only by absolute condensation of background can the story's essentially internal, psychological action

95

come into relief . . . The background will be the texture of sun-baked earth, scorched leaves and grass, stone walls, or the blue wattle sides of the hut." As for the style of photography (for which a Polish cameraman, Mieczysław Jahoda, had been engaged), Wajda noted: "I see this film in flat, uncontrasted images, angled to bring out the texture of objects, with a minimum depth of focus, the background being suggested rather than shown."[1] So much for Wajda's intentions, clear enough, as we can see, before the actual shooting began. Were they bound to come unstuck amid the trials and tribulations he encountered?

Recalling the making of *Gates to Paradise*, Wajda mentioned some of these headaches: "I had no contact with the actors, and what's more I knew next to nothing about working with children. They would say something, but I had no way of checking what it was. There was some kind of barrier between me and the crew, and in the end I found myself just desperately doing my best not to hold things up."[2] "Because of the foreign language," he said on another occasion, "you feel as though you are working in the dark. You begin to suspect that the people around you—the electricians, the assistants—always know better and have more of a clue about the film than you do."[3] "Apart from this, the shooting schedule was extremely tight, and to all intents and purposes the whole film was shot in a single spot. As a result it lacks a vital element: there is no sense of peregrination, of a continuous movement forward . . . With some films you find everything going like a house on fire: the crew is keen, the ideas are there for the asking, there's a feeling of optimism and success on the set. *Gates to Paradise* was the very opposite: from the word go nothing went right."[4] Wajda considers the film a complete write-off.

The story takes place during the span of only a few hours and its principals are the children: Jacques of Cloyers, the shepherd boy who had the original vision; Alexis, a young knight; fifteen-year-old Maud; the slightly older Blanche; and Robert, a miller's son in love with Maud. Dominating them is a Franciscan friar who has joined the crusade and is now, one by one, hearing their confessions. From these there emerges a picture of children in whom the most important quality is missing: the purity of heart which was to have been the strength of the expedition. Instead they are driven by such motives as a craving for power, lust and jealousy. Jacques himself, the instigator of the crusade, turns out to be a creature totally warped by morbid ambition; he also attracts the sexual advances of Ludovic de Vendôme, Count of Chartres and Blois. Interpolated with the confessions is the monologue of the Franciscan, the only

Left: Mathieu Carrière and Pauline Challoner. Right: producer Sam Waynberg, John Fordyce (Jacob) and Wajda during production of GATES TO PARADISE

lucid member of the group, who sees through the whole affair. In these musings we catch echoes of his temptations and doubts, and there is a balancing of points of view, attitudes and ideas.

Wajda adhered fairly closely to Andrzejewski's story, but one gains the impression that he was not altogether convinced by its moral and existential strands; at any rate, he failed to use any of them as an axis for the film. Although this may have been due to the *contretemps* by which it was plagued, the fact remains that it lacks a clear sense of direction, which may also be why the narration keeps faltering and shuddering to a standstill. To make matters worse, the visual style, by which Wajda had set so much store, also emerged patchily. "I followed the script too blindly," he has admitted; "I assumed that the amorality of the liaison between the boy and the Count would have the resounding ring of real drama. I was wrong. At the same time the thing that I was looking for in the subject—the cruelty of a picture of children trying to do adults' work in setting the world to rights—simply failed to come across at all. The moral issues were barely scratched."[5] Wajda has brooded time and again over why the film failed. In 1968, shortly after its ill-starred *première,* he said: "If this film had been made in Poland, it might have had a slightly different meaning . . . Perhaps it would have been more of a political film? The first draft of Andrzejewski's script had an opening which lent the story more of a political than a religious slant. At any rate the exaltation was examined in political rather than religious terms. It showed the clerics confronting the alternative of whether to dispatch the children to a certain death or save them. But their minds didn't work along the moral lines of it being wrong if the children perish and right if they are rescued. They looked at things from the angle of the Church's interests. They were ready to sacrifice the children since this might awaken a desire for vengeance which could become a real force. I think a film with this sort of meaning would have a different significance in Poland than in Yugoslavia or England."[6] Later still, in 1972, Wajda observed that he had a chance of making a film about "contestation" *avant la lettre,* about events which shortly after the film was completed were to start hitting the headlines: the revolt of youth putting into practice certain adult ideas that have proved too much for those who profess them.

The fact is that all of Wajda's films derive their power from the way they have joined in or even triggered off some significant debate—historical, ideological, or social. *Gates to Paradise,* on the other hand, based as it was on a hauntingly-written, extremely intelligent but slightly timeless story, was not only a limp piece of film-making, but worst of all a completely damp squib as far as striking any contemporary sparks was concerned.

It is a film that remains virtually unknown. Apart from the occasional specialised showing—one in London, another in Paris, a third at the West Berlin festival in 1968—it has never come into contact with a normal audience. "Thank God," says Wajda.

13. Stock-Taking—*Everything for Sale*

BETWEEN 1968 AND 1970 Wajda was hardly off the set. Never before in his entire career had he gone through an equally feverish period. In just over two years he directed four feature films, an hour-long TV film, staged two plays (Dürrenmatt's *Play Strindberg* at the "Współczesny" Theatre in Warsaw, and Dostoyevski's *The Possessed* at the "Stary" Theatre in Kraków), and also a TV production of "Macbeth" for good measure. Was this burst of activity by a film-maker with a reputation for picking and choosing his subjects a pure coincidence? "I'm making one film after another," he himself likes to quip, "on the off-chance that one of them will at last come off!"

Fifteen years after his *début* Wajda had come to the point at which an artist begins to take stock of his work and himself. By this time he had a crystallised and generally consistent image in the eyes of both critics and audiences. His name was associated not only with certain themes but also with a certain way of speaking: he talked about the recent history of his country in the tones reserved for use about ourselves, with that typical mixture of strident deprecation and unfeigned pride, owning up to our faults, but also preening ourselves on them. Perhaps he had become a prisoner of his themes, and his obsessions with national cross-purposes. Perhaps it was time for some thorough heart-searching.

After the storm which had raged over *Ashes* and the *débâcle* of *Gates to Paradise*, Wajda began to think of making a film that would be a cross-examination of both himself and his art. The trigger was the tragic death of Zbigniew Cybulski, the Maciek of *Ashes and Diamonds*; on January 8, 1967, late as usual, he tried to jump on a Warsaw train pulling out of Wrocław, but missed his footing and was run over. The death of this extraordinarily popular actor stunned the whole country, and no one more than Wajda, who was not only a personal friend but the director who had given him his first break and major role. "I always wanted to make films with Zbyszek Cybulski," he said in the autumn of 1967, when *Everything for Sale* (*Wszystko na sprzedaż*) was on the floor. "He appeared in only three of my films, but I had also wanted to have him in *Innocent Sorcerers* and *Kanał*. I saw that Zbyszek was not just an actor, but a personality who deserves to be put on the screen as he is, without shoving a role at him.

Wajda and Elżbieta Czyżewska during the filming of
EVERYTHING FOR SALE

He should have played himself. I happened to be in London with some friends at the time, and was mulling over the possibility of such a film about Zbyszek, swapping various anecdotes we could build it round, when Polański rang up with the news that he was dead. I suddenly felt like an author robbed of his hero. It struck me that, no matter what, a film ought to be made about someone as fascinating as he was, even though he was gone . . . I've roughed out a script. The only way of doing it is to show his footprints—I mean, I can't use his name, or his photographs or scenes from his films. In any case, who knows whether Zbyszek wasn't capable of even greater things. I've always felt that he still had in front of him the one-and-only film which would set the seal on what he was, on the character who lived in our midst. The people in my film will follow his tracks, they'll come across the stories circulating about him, the odds and ends of his existence, the places still warm from his presence. He had invaded their lives—our lives!—and in some way thrown them off balance. We were always aware of his assertiveness, his impetuosity. Everyone who worked with him could feel that here was a remarkably stimulating personality who had an astonishing flair for thinking up any number of riveting bits of business, though sometimes we found that on the screen they fell flat, that the exhilaration failed to get across. But everyone liked to work with him because there was something of the fantastic about him. That's how I hope he will come across in the film."[1]

Cybulski's death was, in fact, more than the loss of a friend. Ever since his unforgettable performance in *Ashes and Diamonds* he had personified a certain generation of Poles and a certain stance in life—and also an artistic constellation of which Wajda was one of the leading spirits. His death brought down the curtain on one current in the Polish cinema. The accident in Wrocław brought Wajda face to face, therefore, with the

Film-within-a-film: Beata Tyszkiewicz and Elżbieta Czyżewska

101

question: Where now? As a result *Everything for Sale,* which begins with a shot of someone falling under a train—a stage death, it soon transpires, part of a film-within-a-film—is primarily a picture about the art of cinema, about all the doubts, torments and humiliations as well as joys that Wajda has experienced in the course of his career.

The fact that the impulse behind *Everything for Sale* was the death of a friend of the director, and that it was about the making of a film (and therefore knitted from his personal, almost intimate experiences), gave rise to the suggestion that it should be regarded as a *film à clef* with cryptic and deliberately oblique allusions to incidents in the life of the author and his set, thus making sense only to a narrow in-group. Nothing could be more unfair either to the film or the public. No key is needed to *Everything for Sale,* which lives its own life, in no need of anyone else's reflected glory.

Film-within-a-film: Elżbieta Czyżewska, (opposite),
and below, her fake suicide watched by Andrzej Łapicki

Opposite and below: the Warsaw film world at play

It is a self-contained work, and must be viewed as such. It is not in its biographical details, in its anecdotes, in its echoes of, or quotes from, real life, but within its own frame of reference, in the story it tells, in the themes it broaches and questions it asks, that its relevances must be sought.

An actor has failed to turn up for a scene in a film in which he was to fall under a train on Wrocław station. The director, players and crew are all on edge: what has become of him? The action centres on a handful of principals: Andrzej, the director (Andrzej Łapicki); his wife, Beata (Beata Tyszkiewicz), who was once married to the missing actor; Ela (Elżbieta Czyżewska), an actress and his present wife; and Daniel (Daniel Olbrychski), a rising young actor who is acquiring a popularity among the younger generation similar to the missing man's and is eager to step into his shoes. Mingling with them there is a clutch of actors playing themselves; Bogumił

The actor as director: Łapicki plays Andrzej

Kobiela (who was Cybulski's closest friend), Elżbieta Kępińska, Irena Laskowska, Wajda's assistants in the role of assistant directors, Wojciech Solarz, Andrzej Kostenko, Witold Holtz, and so on. The first half of the film is taken up with their search for the star; the second part is their attempt to answer the questions: What are they to do with the film they have started? How are they to discharge their twin obligations of loyalty to the dead and duty to the living? and What is a director's responsibility for the things he wants or ought to say? These queries are explicitly Andrzej's, but they lie at the back of the minds of everyone involved.

Everything for Sale has, therefore, a lucid, double-decker structure based on two simple points of departure: first, the disappearance of the actor, and then, when they learn of his death, the decision to go ahead with the film even though a vital link has been lost. In each part the events and principals are moving in a clearly-stated direction, and run into obstacles. The

Elżbieta Czyżewska and Andrzej Łapicki

action strung on these two threads builds up into a precisely logical sequence and forms a tight-knit dramatic fabric.

In spite of this simplicity of the general structure, however, there are certain convolutions and meanderings. Within each part there are episodes whose dramatic emphasis and emotional voltage is so intense that they seem to dominate. The temperature of each passage also keeps changing, but the thrust is continually forwards. It is like someone venturing into unknown and forbidding territory, stopping after each step to look around and only then taking the next.

"Looking around" seems, in fact, to be the operative word. Hitherto, Wajda, especially in *Kanal, Ashes and Diamonds* and *Ashes,* had been the kind of artist who works with a fully-created world, in which each gesture, each camera movement, each detail of the *décor* has been shaped by his hand; the force of the picture was generated not so much by the natural-

107

ness and directness of the imagery, as by its expressive significance, symbolism, and visual fascination. In *Everything for Sale* the direction seems to be guided by a different principle. It is less strained and obtrusive, and more reliant on observation and improvisation, as though Wajda was doing no more than scanning a slice of reality and trying to register its attraction, meaning and symbolism; instead of creating it, simply discovering it in its contours, in its unexpected features. This new way of patterning a film is apparent not only in the *mise-en-scène* and the cinematography, but even more so in the playing. Wajda assembled a cast—Elżbieta Czyżewska, Beata Tyszkiewicz, Andrzej Łapicki, Daniel Olbrychski and the rest—who had known Cybulski and so were acting under the same impulse as he was.*

For an interesting discussion of the film and the real-life relationships between the cast and Cybulski, see the article by Colin McArthur, 'Everything for Sale,' in "Sight and Sound," Summer 1969, pp. 139–41.

Andrzej as epic director

Wajda during shooting of EVERYTHING FOR SALE,
with Daniel Olbrychski at left

Thus, they built their parts not only out of their professional know-how, but also from their own private experience. This is an important point in defining the style of the film. The direction of the actors was as relaxed as the whole production. Rather than impose specific gestures and interpretations, Wajda listened to the proposals they dredged out of real life, which he then sifted, modified and stitched together into the material of his narration.

Everything for Sale is, of course, something more than the story either of the search for a missing man (part one) or of the making of a film (part two). Both halves have deeper undercurrents. The star of a film fails to appear on the set, the day's shooting has to be called off, and two people, his present and his former wife, set off on an attempt to run him to earth. This tour and reconnaissance of various *milieus* is not only a

Re-enactment of a real-life incident, as Olbrychski leaps from the train

quest for someone who has disappeared, but also an endeavour to piece together his identity. Gradually certain lines begin to emerge, enigmatic and contradictory, bare glimpses of the personality of a magnificent actor who was apparently also something of a mountebank, who commanded the affection and admiration of those who knew him, but tried their patience as well, who was forever living up to the idiosyncrasies he was at such pains to make his own. This laborious reconstruction of an absent person's features seems to have originally been the main theme of the film. In the event, however, no such description ever materialises, any more than an identikit can be assembled from the statements of eye-witnesses. The face remains inscrutable, apart from odd scraps of information which serve only to open up fresh by-ways and shift the focus to the film's other themes.

Beata hears of the actor's death over the car radio

When it is learned that the actor is dead, the prying into the truth is made to seem at the very least ghoulish, if not exactly unnecessary. Death is an occasion for silence and platitudes, for sifting out all the ambiguities in the portrait and pointing up the legend.

The theme of the missing actor does not, however, vanish altogether, but is sublimated and lifted to a moral plane. In place of the earlier tentative delineation there come other questions—about the traces that so hypnotic a figure leaves behind, about the imprint in the memories of those close to him which fades so rapidly, and about the supposedly more durable monument of his art. Quite unexpectedly, therefore, the film is exploring, though not in so many words, the subject of time and evanescence, and from there the matter of life which goes on, which refuses to accept death, which

111

Visual exhilaration: the Warsaw film set at the fairground

insists on its vacuum being filled—in the person of the younger man (Daniel) who moves in on the other's barely-vacated haunts, who puts on the jacket he conveniently kept hanging in the cloakroom of a bar, who re-enacts his favourite scene. All this is recorded ruefully, but unreproachfully. In the conflict between the calls of remembrance and the present, between loyalty to the dead and the necessity of interring him, the victory can only go to life.

Meanwhile, half-way through the film, there comes a new situation posed by the implications of continuing the picture in spite of everything. Here, too, a certain deeper theme quickly develops in a succession of scenes, foreshadowed earlier, which incessantly and often dramatically heighten the contrast between cinema and life (the staged accident, Ela's fake suicide,

"An affirmation of life"

the make-believe of the historical epic, etc.). The effect is a continual shuttle between film and reality. Art and life, illusion and reality, the truth which sparks between them, the quest for this truth, the mechanism of its appearance and disappearance—all these are woven into the second major strand of *Everything for Sale.*

The angle is not, however, the same as in Fellini's *8½ (Otto e mezzo).* For him the drama of the creative process lay chiefly in the impotence of an artist paralysed by a web of dos and don'ts, by his own helplessness, by the leviathan of contemporary civilisation. For Wajda it is not a matter of lost bearings, but of the traumas that come from the attachment, loyalty, discretion and memory owed to the dead; and he discovers similar hang-ups in his players and associates. As he digs deeper into this theme, new ob-

113

jections assail him, all springing from the same source—the morality of artistic creation.

The creative process, the confrontation between fiction and reality, the overcoming of scruples and inhibitions, is found to be morally equivocal. This point is made right at the start when Ela, having completed a harrowing suicide scene, instantly switches to a perfectly matter-of-fact expression and collects her salary. Not that it is merely a question of the money. The film-within-a-film is a sustained act of self-exposure, a public display before an audience of millions, of one's intimate experiences, weaknesses and doubts. In other words, the artist's struggle with his work is always, as far as Wajda is concerned, a moral one.

Hence the tone of bitterness—and the ironic title. The death of the actor and the inevitable process of laying him to rest is communicated bleakly, but without rancour. There is, too, a similar sourness not far short of pain in the dissection of the moral conflicts of creation. It remains, however, well this side of any condemnation of art, which as Wajda sees it is not only a medium, not only form and content, not only a message addressed to the audience, but a process of devouring the artist, sucking in his being, his experiences, and his shame. "The poet," Jean Cocteau once said, "is a man who bleeds; and poetry is the bloodstain by the wayside." Such a romantic view of art (not to mention cinema, where wheeling-and-dealing is so much a part of the game) is a declaration of faith by an artist who treats his medium in the same way as the great poets treated theirs, investing the creative act with a heroic dimension.

Everything for Sale does not offer any precise intellectual conclusions. Wajda is not a philosopher, but he is a genuine artist. All he says is that someone dies and is quickly forgotten—a sad state of affairs, but the truth. Film is a mixture of reality and fiction, and the creative process demeaning and mortifying; this is another thing that one must learn to live with. And when, at the moment of supreme disarray, a herd of horses appears on the horizon and Daniel begins running delightedly alongside, the only thing left is to train the camera in their direction and track with this fit of abandon to the very end. It is an affirmation of life, come what may, and of beauty above all things.

14.   A Shot at Comedy—*Hunting Flies*

"I'VE ALWAYS THOUGHT that the really difficult thing is to make a funny film. The proof of whether you're a good or bad director seems to me to be whether you can produce something that's funny. Since testing yourself isn't exactly pleasant (as you never know how it will come out), I took a long time making up my mind that a film like that might be right for me."[1] Whether or not Wajda really wanted to see if his talent ran to comedy, it is certain that after *Everything for Sale,* which had been a particularly nerve-racking experience because of the desperate gamble in both subject and treatment, he was anxious for a radical change. Comedy offered a new field—and a chance to replenish his tools and personal image. He saw that his *oeuvre,* rich and ostensibly varied though it was, had in fact an amazing uniformity of content and form. Two, perhaps three, films could be found, like *Innocent Sorcerers,* which had, at least on the surface, a different dramatic structure, style and emotional temperature, though even they bore the invisible stamp of his favourite themes. Already in *Everything for Sale* one could sense a nagging query that he might have gone over the same ground once too often, that if he did not strike out into fresh fields, he would be overtaken by the younger men. It was therefore a dramatic attempt at renovation. Now he was eager to repeat the exercise in a lighter vein.

As it happened, television had been eager for some time for him to make a film, and the end of 1968 found him, therefore, in the right frame of mind to take up the offer. He chose a script by Stanisław Lem, Poland's most accomplished science fiction author, which was a slightly over-stretched spoof on the subject of transplants, then very much in the news, about a racing driver continually involved in fatal accidents and having some vital part replaced each time until finally he has undergone a complete mutation. Although quickly made and confined to a few skeletal, futuristic sets, the film was a lively affair, racing from one hilarious twist to another, and played with a rich sense of the grotesque, especially by Bogumił Kobiela in the main role.* *Roly-Poly (Przekładaniec)* was, therefore, slapstick sci-

---

*By a grisly irony life imitated art: Kobiela died in a car crash a few months after completing the film, and only two years after the tragic death of his closest friend, Zbigniew Cybulski.

ence fiction, and farce being entirely new territory for Wajda, it had its detractors as well as admirers. For Wajda, however, it was no more than an extravaganza, hardly worth a second thought. He was really searching for a normal full-length screen comedy, and not a short television skit.

His attention was caught by Janusz Głowacki's story "Hunting Flies," printed in the weekly "Kultura." "It was only after reading Głowacki's piece," he has said, "that I decided the right moment had probably come to have a stab at something funny with a good chance of bringing it off."[2] A writer and journalist, Janusz Głowacki had published in 1968 a collection of stories entitled "A Whirligig of Nonsense" ("Wirówka nonsensu"), which took an astringent look at Warsaw's "smart set." Born in 1938, he was one of a generation of writers beginning to make their mark in the late Sixties. "Hunting Flies" contained all his hallmarks: intelligent observation, acid humour, a sense of the absurd, knitted into a satirical picture of middle-class attitudes and bohemian snobberies.

Wajda followed Głowacki's script fairly closely. *Hunting Flies (Polowanie na muchy)* is about Włodek (Zygmunt Malanowicz), an ex-language student

Richard Fox (Bogumił Kobiela) with his psychiatrist, Dr. Benglow (Piotr Wysocki) in ROLY-POLY (below); Wajda rehearsing a scene for HUNTING FLIES (opposite)

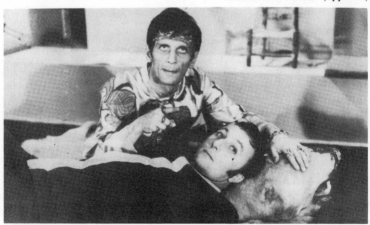

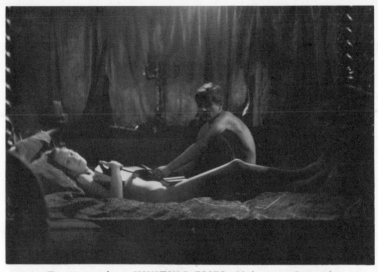

Two scenes from HUNTING FLIES: Małgorzata Braunek and Zygmunt Malanowicz

*HUNTING FLIES: above, Malanowicz and Braunek;
below, Wajda directing the party sequence*

fed up with the stifling atmosphere of his home life (wife, son, mother- and father-in-law, the eternally blaring television) who is looking for adventure. He finds it in the arms of an attractive young student, Irena (Małgorzata Braunek). She, however, falls in love not so much with Włodek for himself, as with the writer *manqué* she believes she has discovered and means to lick into shape. She takes over his affairs, and via studio, editorial office, and the modish meeting-place of the lions of the literary world, launches him on the scene. All in vain. Irena cannot see that Włodek is simply not capable, and the fires she has stoked in him quickly fizzle out. The thread between them snaps, and he returns home, only to find an alarming change: his dowdy, suburban wife has suddenly developed high-flown ambitions of her own—with him, against cast, as hero.

The characterisations of the girl and wife, and of the other female cameos, such as an imperious lady editor, made some critics believe that Wajda was taking a vicious swipe at aggressive women hell-bent on setting up a matriarchy, and they detected a strong streak of misogyny in the film. The critic of the weekly "Polityka" even went so far as to track down links with the old "Polish school": "Wajda broaches an issue which has been bobbing around for a long time and is typical of his generation: mesmerisation by the female. As we know, the theme of our 'lost generation' has run through our art in two stages: the first was the trauma of defeat, the second the emotional paralysis in subsequent, everyday life brought on by the historical disaster which warped normal heroes."[3]

I doubt, however, that any such complexities were either intended by Wajda or found their way into the film. With the benefit of hindsight this is even more obvious. *Hunting Flies* is merely a *divertissement,* the Pygmalion-Galatea theme in reverse, with the man in the fashioned role. Certainly it is spiked with gibes and cautionary tales about female aggressiveness, blended with a caricatured picture of Warsaw in the late Sixties; equally plainly, however, there is no clear-cut moral, no final QED. To read intended profundities into Wajda's film (an attack on matriarchy, on the literary world even) and then to demolish them as glib and superficial, was a tactic as devious as it was self-defeating.

The only fair question is about the quality of this *divertissement.* What type of humour did Wajda represent in revealing this hidden side of his personality? Whatever else it may be, it is not light, subtle or understated.

Opposite: Włodek free from the pressures of home

In all his films Wajda had made a point of emphatic, heightened effects; he had little time for the delicate touch, for hints. His first comedy shows a similar preference for the bludgeon rather than the rapier. In the gamut of humour this means caricature, and *Hunting Flies* is exactly that, especially in its drawing of the central characters: a man-eater preying on a stolid, clod-footed, feckless booby. Because Włodek is such an unprepossessing figure, the film is cold. For all that, Wajda took one step further the metamorphosis of style shown in *Everything for Sale*. Both the photography and *mise-en-scène* are casual, uncontrived and very "modern," totally unburdened by portentous symbolism, and the performances, with Wajda's outstanding "discovery" Małgorzata Braunek, are relaxed, natural and spontaneous.

The film passed relatively unnoticed at Cannes and had a mixed reception at home. The critics who had supported Wajda throughout his career were not amused, and there were disgruntled murmurs that such tomfoolery was no way for a director of his stature to be carrying on. Those who had so often castigated him were, on the other hand, rather inclined to approve. The perennial Wajda debate was in this case relatively subdued; only shortly afterwards did it really break out with redoubled fury.

Voracious womanhood—the final image of HUNTING FLIES

15. Love and 'Polishness'
—Landscape after the Battle

AFTER *HUNTING FLIES*—no more than a diversion in Wajda's *oeuvre*, and of greater interest as an exercise in a different key and a fresh field than as a film in its own right—he returned to home ground: the Polish experience, the stance, the dilemmas and conflicts of his countrymen at a critical juncture in their country's history. Shades of *Ashes and Diamonds?* The resemblances between *Ashes and Diamonds* and *Landscape after the Battle* (*Krajobraz po bitwie*) are unmistakeable: the same fateful year, 1945, when a Rubicon had to be crossed on the frontier of two ages; and a similar kind of hero, lacerated by the war, stumbling upon a brief, intense love which breaks down his bitterness and kindles hopes of a new beginning. In both films the encounter ends tragically: just as the shell of disillusion is beginning to crack, there arrives a senseless, fortuitous death. Thus, in each film can be seen the two major themes which have formed the bearings of Wajda's cinema: love and "Polishness."

Translating Borowski to the screen presented problems quite different and far more awkward than *Ashes and Diamonds*. Andrzejewski's novel was tightly constructed, crowded with character and incident, and conventional in its dramatic twists; it offered an arresting and sympathetically-drawn hero in a succession of scenes sketched with great verve and sweep. It burrowed deep into a specific moment in history and created an autonomous world.

Borowski's work, on the other hand, is totally out of the ordinary, a unique phenomenon in the whole of postwar European literature. A writer who published his first pieces during the Occupation, he was deported to the concentration camp at Auschwitz. One of the survivors, he set down after the war his experiences in two small collections of stories, which provoked considerable discussion. He was accused of a-humanism when he described with icy detachment cannibalism among the prisoners; when he observed with the imperturbability of an entomologist the same reactions, the same monstrous reflexes in his friends and in himself as in the executioners; when he noted almost off-handedly how, during a game of football, he had twice taken a corner kick and happened to notice *between one kick and the next* several thousand people being exterminated in the adjoining

Daniel Olbrychski . . .

sector. "Ladies and Gentlemen, to the Gas Chamber" ("Proszę państwa, do gazu") is the title of one of these pieces and it conveys the essence of his writing. "A World Hewn out of Stone" ("Swiat ciosany w kamieniu")— the phrase is Borowski's, but it was adopted by the critics to designate the work of this astonishing prodigy, a harrowing record of "the age of furnaces" that was also a supremely penetrating analysis of what came to be called the "univers concentrationnaire." Anyone like Borowski who had lived through it was for ever, in a phrase quoted earlier, "contaminated by death." He himself was no exception: in 1951 he committed suicide.

The germ of the film was a story entitled "The Battle of Grünwald" ("Bitwa pod Grunwaldem"), which Wajda enlarged upon with his assistant director, Andrzej Brzozowski. In both content and tone it departs somewhat from Borowski's usual *ambiance*; at any rate, it lacks on the surface the

. . . as Tadeusz in the concentration camp

ultimate situations of his Auschwitz fiction. The setting is just after the war in a American D.P.s camp in Germany, full of Polish refugees: freed prisoners-of-war, former forced labour deportees and concentration camp survivors. Quartered in an old German barracks, they seem to be in the grip of some fever, squabbling over soup, bread, a radio—but also over patriotism and politics. All of them, whatever their lot before they arrived in the camp, have to make up their minds about events in Poland: they must either return forthwith or burn their bridges behind them. The climax comes in a furious brawl which breaks out during the performance of a bizarre pageant called "The Battle of Grünwald" (a re-enactment of the Polish victory over the Teutonic Knights in the Fifteenth century). All this was described with irony, anger and venom; the dramas involved, how-ever, are obviously of a different order from those of the concentration

125

camp stories. Nevertheless, there is a clear thread linking the two. Although "The Battle of Grünwald" takes place in a normal (not a "stone") world, it is regarded through the eyes of a man who has looked upon that other one, who has been "there." The point of the story lies not in the accuracy of its observation of behaviour and psychology, but in the perspective of someone who has images like "ramp," "furnace," and "block" burned into his memory, who has become as impassive as, to quote Borowski, "a tree and a stone, and as mute as a felled tree and a hewn stone."

"The Battle of Grünwald" gave Wajda, therefore, the raw material of plot and conflict, but no central character, since his features were scattered among all the other stories or even, perhaps, submerged in the biography

Olbrychski and Tadeusz Janczar (Karol)

of their author. A sharply-delineated figure was needed if the film was to have coherence and direction, so Wajda supplied a young writer and intellectual called Tadeusz (Daniel Olbrychski), a figure who does not actually appear in Borowski's first-person narratives, but whose presence can be felt on every page—a projection of the author himself. In fact, this solution was nothing like as obvious as it appears, since not only was it a matter of fleshing out Tadeusz, but of seeing things from his point of view, a man who is burned out, proof against all emotive mumbo-jumbo, and belligerently peering at everyone and everything in the hope of finding common traits and feelings. No easy task, and where the film falters it is possibly due to the alternatives between which Wajda was slung: either the cold, merciless, analytical vision of Borowski, or the heated, emotional currents latent in the events and, above all, in the protagonist, in his psyche, in his metamorphosis from apathy to pain, and from imperviousness to self-definition. Wajda chose the second course, and *Landscape* can therefore only be called a film built from the material of "The Battle of Grünwald," not a transposition of Borowski's universe. An artist with so individual a make-up was entitled to use only the things which allowed him to remain himself.

The film opens with a long sequence showing the liberation of a concentration camp. Though perfectly realistic, it has something of the look of ballet or mime—a seemingly aimless scramble in the spotless snow of figures in striped uniforms dashing around among the barbed wire—but in fact forms a capsule image of a certain state of mind: exhilaration mixed with bewilderment and apprehension. This is cross-cut with the trampling to death of a *kapo*—an episode taken from Borowski's "Silence" ("Milczenie"). Here already, in the contrast between the sententious, well-meaning, but pathetic speech of the liberator who has seen nothing and the savage, wordless reaction of people who have seen everything, there is struck the first of the jarring notes which regularly punctuate the film. Little is said in this sequence; only Vivaldi's music lends it a tranquil, harmonious, human flavour. Tadeusz can be glimpsed in the crowd, a figure apart, sullen and indifferent.

After this prelude the film switches to the D.P.s camp with its wrangles, parades, prayers, and meals. A whole episode devoted to Tadeusz being sentenced to solitary confinement is directed with gusto and a touch of caricature, which suggests a different kind of film from the one promised by the opening prelude and, for that matter, delivered later. Inconsistency of style? Perhaps; but these scenes serve to bring Tadeusz gradually into

127

Rapture and death: Stanisława Celińska with Olbrychski . . .

focus, and it is only when we fasten on him that *Landscape after the Battle* begins to become the moving film it is.

The grip is tightened with the appearance of Nina (Stanisława Celińska), a fugitive from Poland. In the encounter between these two worn-out, embittered figures, somewhat taken aback by each other, there appears the main theme of Wajda's film—love. It surfaces in the poignant dialogue which begins back in the barracks and develops in the course of a long stroll among trees and slag-heaps, in the unexpected scenery of normal existence. Their exchanges are disjointed, tongue-tied, by turns snappish and tender, with a distinct undertow of physical desire, but very innocent and self-conscious. It is only now that the characters, especially Tadeusz, begin to fill out. Daniel Olbrychski, a popular actor, made this part his first fully mature role, while Stanisława Celińska lent hers a remarkable

128

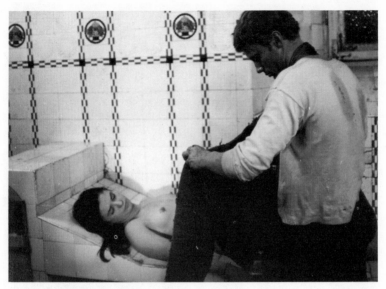

. . . in LANDSCAPE AFTER THE BATTLE

vitality and power. Up to this point Tadeusz has been a stock figure: with his wire-rimmed spectacles, his books, his air of aloofness and unconcern, he might have been a stereotype of "the intellectual amid the hurly-burly of war." In these sequences, however, the heart of the character emerges. Beneath the crust of irony, he is a wounded being and, like all such, aggressive, prickly, and ready to lash out. Human solidarity? National loyalties? Principle, comradeship, love? For someone who has been "there," all the values of the ancient humanist tradition seem cloying and hypocritical. These undertones come over most clearly in his desultory dialogue with the girl, but there are others, more muted but audible—the awakening of an embarassed, unwelcome, almost rebuffed longing for love, life, and affirmation.

When the girl is killed, unnecessarily and pointlessly, his first reaction is

129

Tadeusz clutches his beloved books

to give way again to that tide of virulent rage. "Never mind," he tells an American officer, who wrings his hands over her death in syrupy horror, "you've shot a girl from a camp. Here in Europe we're used to that." When, however, he sees the yellowing corpse of the girl in a mortuary or bath-house with the sickening look of an *abattoir,* an animal howl bursts out of him. It is a sign that the crust of indifference, disgust and despair is cracking, the first intimation after a grave disease of a return to life and escape from the tundra of death. A film about love, certainly, for here love is shown as a potent force regenerating human nature, the individual's last line of defence against petrification.

What of the other major theme of *Landscape*? Let us consider the sequence of the Grünwald pageant, which Tadeusz watches at the moment when his grief over the girl is at its height. Highly-charged visually, the scene is at once grisly, ludicrous and stirring, but consummates the theme of "Polishness." In Borowski it came at a different stage in the story and, in any case, had a different meaning: for Wajda, however, it fitted with a recurring *motif* in his cinema. It is possible that this particular scene most engrossed him in the reading, and it may even have been the reason he decided to make this disaster-courting film in the first place. It is, in the event, the most stunning passage—and the one most likely in Poland to touch exposed nerves. A mixture of the sublime and the ridiculous, pain and pleasure, the grotesque and the beautiful, this way of speaking about "Polishness," about its traditions, beliefs and myths, runs through the whole of Wajda's *oeuvre*. That dawn *polonaise* in *Ashes and Diamonds,* the troopers charging the tanks in *Lotna,* many of the scenes in *Ashes* were pitched in this same key. They were accused of mixing values and garbling tradition. What is more, this emotional confusion led critics to complain in one case that he had not denounced certain aspects of history and in another that he had blackened them. Meanwhile, Wajda remained, as always, in this same state of emotional ambiguity, teetering between derision and enthusiasm. Desecrating and extolling this "Polishness" by turns, he was following in the footsteps of Słowacki and Norwid, Żeromski and Wyspiański, the writers and poets of the Romantic tradition he has always invoked. They had attacked this theme with the same blend of rage and love, torn equally between affirmation and criticism. No writer in this lineage ever submitted "Polishness" to cold and devastating analysis; nor did any, on the other hand, truckle to it with great relish. It may be that the whole concept and the argument over it that has absorbed Polish literature for almost two centuries should be dismissed as totally sterile. The historian of culture must, however, admit that it is this particular theme, so incongruous in European art, which has given birth to the most passionate and vibrant works in the Polish heritage; they and no others are the ones which have echoed loudest and struck the most resonant chords in the public mind.

For this very reason *Landscape* triggered yet another vehement public debate. Basically it was the same dispute as the ones over *Kanal, Ashes and Diamonds* and *Ashes,* but this time the issue was not side-tracked by historical and literary arguments; as a result it had the sharper ring of straight ideological and political controversy.

From one corner came the indignant tirades of all those who saw the film as an affront to "Polishness," an attack on the virtue, nobility and wisdom of the Polish nation. Once again, they protested, the Poles had been denigrated. "The Polish people in *Landscape*," wrote Maciej Wierzyński, "are made up entirely of hysterical idiots who for reasons known only to themselves mope around under the eye of the Americans rather than return to Poland."[1] This was by no means an extremist view; there was even sharper invective in the air, coupled with ill-disguised demands that the film should be withdrawn, or at any rate banned from exhibition abroad where it might create "a bad impression" (in fact the film was released in Poland *after* being shown in Cannes, where it did not, for that matter, fare as well as had been hoped).

Baroque pageantry: the "Battle of Grünwald" is performed at the climax of LANDSCAPE AFTER THE BATTLE

On the other side were those, the majority of film critics among them, who made clear their appreciation not just of one particular picture or Wajda's cinema as such, but of a certain way of thinking and viewing one's country and one's nation—without violent flag-waving, with an awareness not only of its *grandeurs,* but also of the grotesque, shabby and cruel elements in its make-up. This was the stance that Wajda had adopted in all his key works. It was, therefore, as it had been five years before, an argument not about a film nor about Wajda, but about ideological imponderables. The point was very dramatically made by the Grand Old Man of Polish letters and journalism, Melchior Wańkowicz, himself a "veteran," a one-time *émigré,* who might have been expected to feel personally stung and offended by *Landscape.* Instead, he wrote a trenchant article under the eloquent title, "The Teeth of My Heart": "Unless the scurvy scab . . . is scraped off this nation which has the virtues of a flexible culture, it will become a trampled gangway, a nonentity. You [must not] spit contemptuously on this scab . . . you must dig your nails into it and tear. Like Wajda does."[2]

Wajda shares a joke with Olbrychski during the shooting of
LANDSCAPE AFTER THE BATTLE

133

16. Eros and Thanatos—*The Birch-Wood*

MEANWHILE TELEVISION, its production capacity continually growing, had again been courting Wajda for a full-length feature. *The Birch-Wood* (*Brzezina*), which was the result, is in no way a television film; it went in fact into normal theatrical release and was chosen to represent Polish cinema at the Moscow International Film Festival.

Wajda, who had in the past battened on such a variety of fiction, turned in this case to one of Poland's most distinguished writers, Jarosław Iwaszkiewicz, already prominent in the *Avant-garde* of the Twenties and still remarkably prolific for his years. Though the cinema has been chary of tackling his writing, it has inspired one of its finest creations, Jerzy Kawalerowicz's *Mother Joan of the Angels* (*Matka Joanna od Aniołów*). Why had Wajda, so eager to quarry the best in literature, never previously been attracted to his work? Was this great writer's imagination, sensibility and *persona* too far removed from his own?

The original story was written in 1932 and ranks as one of the minor masterpieces of its time. Its account of two brothers buried in the solitude of a remote forest brought into focus one of Iwaszkiewicz's recurrent preoccupations: the theme of death, of life overshadowed by intimations of death, or—to put it in existentialist terms—the ubiquity of death in the structures of life. The only way, and at the same time the most natural one, of standing up to death, he seems to say, lies in romantic and physical love. Though love had appeared in *Siberian Lady Macbeth,* in *Ashes and Diamonds,* and in *Landscape after the Battle* as a force which could redeem from death, which regenerated human nature, these films never took on the makings of total existentialist dramas. In this respect *The Birch-Wood* is unique.

The action is set during the Thirties in the lodge of a forest warden, Bolesław (Daniel Olbrychski), whose brother has returned home after several years of treatment for tuberculosis in Switzerland. The film is the story of his dying and of the strained relationship between the two brothers, bedevilled by the teasing presence of a village girl. Robust and healthy though he is, Bolesław seems to carry the contagion of death. His wife has

Opposite: Wajda on location for THE BIRCH-WOOD

Daniel Olbrychski as Bolesław

died a year earlier, her body lies in the birch-wood, and he has been left alone with a small daughter, Ola. Were there some accounts unsettled between him and his wife? Does something still fester in his system? In contrast, Stanisław (Olgierd Łukaszewicz), though his life is running out (he has come to the birch-wood to die), bubbles with zest and sexual vitality, and is soon pursuing Malina (Emilia Krakowska), who is the very embodiment of the life force. But although this affair enables Stanisław to savour a fulfilment he has never known before, it awakens in Bolesław feelings of jealousy and hatred which unexpectedly develop into a fierce desire for the girl. After a temporary improvement, Stanisław dies, Malina is about to marry a village lad, and Bolesław leaves his forest hermitage with his daughter. All that remains are two lonely crosses in the birch-wood.

Iwaszkiewicz penetrates, in the psychological clashes, to the deeper layer

136

of an existentialist drama. Wajda has followed this lead, developed the theme and pushed it further. There is no escape from death except in the consummation of the *libido*—love becomes a source of life, the one great force which can counteract the death instinct. Here, to use Freudian terminology, is an opposition between the life urge and the death urge, between Eros and Thanatos. The duel fought out in the birch-wood is between these two drives.

Eros and Thanatos: seeking the right visual key for this conflict, Wajda once again turned to painting, this time to the work of an artist similarly fascinated by this subject, Jacek Malczewski, an *art nouveau* painter recently rescued from oblivion. The theme of Eros and Thanatos was something of an obsession with this extremely prolific artist who left behind approximately 2,000 canvasses. His painting, "Thanatos," was loaned by

Emilia Krakowska as Malina (right) with the old housekeeper, Katarzyna

the National Museum in Warsaw and hung in the forester's lodge, where it seems to preside over the drama and, like a tuning fork, establish the film's tone, shading and temperature.

The colour is certainly eerie, ugly in its way, "cadaverous" as it was called—a *mélange* of putrid yellows, greens and violets. These tones dominate the photography of human bodies with their faces splodged by sickly, sinister stains. The use of the same spectrum as Malczewski lent the film's images a disquieting, misty, but ever-present air of disease, decomposition and death. On the other hand, in the human shapes, in the naturalistic play of muscles, in the poses of figures towering over their surroundings and nature—and this was a recurrent feature in the composition of Malczewski's paintings—there is a clear sense of that vigour and vitality which opposes the deathly pallor of life. Again as with Malczewski, landscape also performs a distinctive function in the film: it is not

Malina and Bolesław (below) and Malina and Stanisław (Olgierd Łukaszewicz) embrace within the all-pervading birch-wood

A rare moment of exhilaration

simply a backdrop—its beauty, harmony and tranquillity act as a balm to the over-wrought characters torn between Eros and Thanatos.

The Birch-Wood was, therefore, carefully tuned to a specific visual style. The photography, art direction, *mise-en-scène*, even the performances, are all made to match. Only Bolesław, who begins with the smell of death and only later manages to shake it off, escapes these baleful hues. His face has the normal tan of a healthy, outdoor man.

Although this film appears at first glance a fleeting, marginal episode in Wajda's *oeuvre*, it marks a milestone in his career. From the outset he had picked subjects which were prickly, which sharply confronted national and social myths, and which argued with history. Here, for the first time, he made a success of a theme both universal and timeless, succeeding where previously defeated (working with a different story and a different kind of

140

Bolesław with his daughter, Ola (Elżbieta Żołek)

writing) in *Gates to Paradise*. To the eternal questions of love and death he brought a new dimension, a new emotional climate, and a fresh dramatic shape. It was for him a very enriching experience.

Nevertheless many critics are inclined to regard *The Birch-Wood* as a cold work, "old-fashioned" in its subject and "square" in visual style. They see it, therefore, as the sign of a crisis in Wajda's cinema, a point of view which is difficult to accept. The film's touch of greatness comes not only from its aesthetic sophistication, its self-imposed restrictions, and concentration on three characters and their shared disquiets—all qualities completely new to Wajda—but above all from his first attempt to wrestle in earnest with the most deep-seated anxieties of human existence which for centuries have been art's most difficult material. Few film-makers have taken up this challenge; fewer still have brought it off.

17. Crucifixion by the Motorway
—Pilate and Others

WHERE DID WAJDA suddenly gain the idea of filming the story of Christ? In 1970 he had been in touch with a West Berlin producer over the possibility of making a medium-length film as an illustration to the music of Krzysztof Penderecki's "Passion according to St. Matthew" ("Pasja według Swiętego Mateusza"). Wajda saw the idea as a semi-documentary picture with three interweaving strands: the sequences of the Mass, the audience and the musicians, and an account of someone dying, which would be a parallel to the other death which forms the subject of the Mass. In the end nothing came of this project, but the theme remained in his mind.

"I once saw a newspaper photograph which I cut out and filed away. It showed three Dutch 'provos,' the one in the middle being the spitting image of Christ and his two companions the thieves. I even thought up the outlines of a script: a child is born in a garage somewhere in Berlin in 1945; thirty years later we see him as a hippie wandering around the country preaching some message."[1] Two Warsaw writers later produced for Wajda a treatment of this subject, incorporating a string of other contemporary analogies (the Evangelists as journalists, Judas as an *agent provocateur*, and so on).

Finally there fell into Wajda's lap the novel "The Master and Margarita" by Mikhail Bulgakov, a Soviet writer (1891–1940) who had, in a sense, been re-discovered in the Sixties following the publication of a number of previously unknown books, among which was this. It is regarded as his masterpiece and he had worked on it for many years, beginning in the Twenties. A moralist and sceptic, Bulgakov produced in "The Master and Margarita" a strange blend of realism and fantasy, set in Moscow in the Twenties among writers, artists, activists, devils and angels. The absurd mingles with the sublime, poignant lyricism with black comedy. Throughout the thirty-three chapters of the novel runs a thread ostensibly unconnected with the main plot: an account of the Passion, though the central figure is not the man Bulgakov calls Jeshua, but the Roman governor, Pontius Pilate. It is related in four chapters scattered around the book like parentheses, and everything, beginning with Jeshua being led before Pilate and ending with the fate of Matthew, has the matter-of-fact air of being all in a day's work. Thus, even the circumstances which bring about Jeshua's crucifixion

Opposite: Matthew (Daniel Olbrychski) with the corpse of Jeshua

Jeshua (Wojciech Pszoniak) is hoisted to the Cross

are perfectly routine: a demarcation dispute between the Sanhedrin and the Roman governor, political horse-trading, the eternal mechanism of police provocation, even the migraine from which Pilate is suffering at the moment he has to issue his decision. What is the point of confronting these events with contemporary motivations? Is it an attempt to find a latter-day key to what took place two thousand years ago or, *vice versa,* is the story of Christ meant to be an allegory about the modern world of today? The Pilate theme works both ways in Bulgakov's novel, but the latter interpretation seems to count for more.

Wajda made *Pilate and Others (Pilatus und Andere/Piłat i inni)* in the autumn of 1971 for the West German Second Channel (Zweites deutsches Fernsehen). It was originally to have been fully "historical," and the exotic scenery of Morocco was proposed for the locations. Subsequently, however, it was decided that it would be entirely shot in the undisguised German landscape—forcing Wajda to re-think the whole concept. Almost the whole of the cast was recruited in Poland (among them Wajda's favourite actors, Daniel Olbrychski and Andrzej Łapicki) and the part of Christ was given to Wojciech Pszoniak, an actor from Kraków who had recently scored a triumph in Wajda's splendid production of Camus's version of Dostoyevski's "The Possessed." The TV-*première* took place on March 29, the Wednesday of Holy Week.

It opens with a short sequence which acts as a prologue, showing a ram entering an *abattoir* followed by a flock of sheep. These are slaughtered, and the ram comes out by another door to bring in the next flock ("Someone told me," Wajda informed me, "that this was standard stockyard practice. Later I found out this wasn't so, but no matter"). A journalist, played by Wajda himself, interviews the ram:

"Is yours a moral job?"

"In a sense you could call me a victim of the system. But there it is—I have a duty to discharge. I'm respected and I don't want to betray the confidence placed in me."

"So you don't see any moral problems about your job?"

"You see, only a free man can be completely moral. In any case I doubt that so great a matter can be immoral."

The story proper now begins. Jeshua (Wojciech Pszoniak) is brought before Pilate (Jan Kreczmar) for interrogation. One by one the other characters appear: Caiaphas (Vladek Sheybal), Afranius the police chief (Andrzej Lapicki), Judas (Jerzy Zelnik) and Matthew (Daniel Olbrychski). When the tragedy has run its course and Jeshua has been crucified, Pilate is overcome by disgust of the whole affair, and especially with Judas; he hints as much to Afranius, who wastes no time in acting: Judas is lured into a trap by a woman (actually a man in drag) and stabbed to death. When Matthew learns from Pilate that Judas is dead, he asks, faithful to Jeshua to the bitter end, for parchment, and later we see him hunched over a typewriter amid way-out contemporary furniture. In the final scene a cross comes into sight, dragged by Matthew down the *Autobahn* against the stream of oncoming traffic.

What is the time and place of these events? Jeshua's interrogation is conducted in the old Nazi stadium in Nuremberg. The Via Dolorosa is the ring road round Frankfurt-am-Main. Golgotha is a giant rubbish tip next to an *Autobahn* near Wiesbaden. Thousands of cars hurtle down the highway as Jeshua is nailed to the cross; none of them stop or slow down.

Jeshua is dressed in a timeless, loose-fitting costume: Christ? hippie? hobo? Afranius, on the other hand, is the epitome of trendy elegance, suspiciously so in the manner of "fuzz." Judas is similarly modish. And Matthew, when he sits down to write the Gospel, is suddenly surrounded by Allen Jones's famous woman-shaped furniture.

Wajda's bold shuffling together of scene, costume and setting—and hence of the co-ordinates of time and space—was a very risky idea, but it paid off abundantly. Everything looks quite natural, almost matter-of-course, so there is little difficulty in suspending disbelief. The film gives the impression of taking place in the wings of some vast theatre where it is in no way surprising to find workmen in overalls rubbing shoulders with Roman centurions, or people conversing about suffering and morality against a backdrop of illusionist scenery or a city sky-line. This is all the easier to accept because of the extreme simplicity of the photography which is almost documentary in style, without any of the poker-work of elaborate shots, significant angles, intricate camera movements, and startling changes of focus. Everything seems, in fact, to have been shot off-the-cuff, like a straightforward piece of *reportage*.

Only the reality created or contrived by the director is strange and paradoxical. For what in the end is the film trying to say? Compared with Bulgakov's novel, its meaning seems to be both broader and narrower. Narrower because Wajda gives the impression of deliberately grinding no axes, arguing no cases, but simply presenting the facts—except that (as with Bulgakov) the point of view is that of Pilate, who thereby becomes a spokesman for we who are alive today and who are continually torn by the conflict between conscience and practical necessities, between a sense of responsibility for the lives of others and the whole world and the temptation of taking the easy way out and "washing our hands." Pilate's stance is, in Wajda's treatment, that of the contemporary man. It is doubtful however, that his film was intended to "demythologise" the story of Christ or, conversely, to shore up the legend with psychological probability and a plausible moral rationale. The title which he chose originally, *A Film for Good Friday* (*Ein Film für Karfreitag/Film na Wielki Piątek*), seems to indicate a sense of neutrality, a paradoxical determination to avoid the strict province of faith and religion. At the same time, however, the film has broader implications. Like *Everything for Sale* it has a wealth of incidental detail, an intensity of episode which sometimes eclipses the story of Christ. Basically it is a series of variations which stem from the Passion, but which rapidly spread in widening ripples to touch on the themes of suffering, betrayal, pain, and the cruelty, past and present, which comes from indifference—and also of art, performance, costume . . .

Doubtless all these intimations, reflections and parallels do not always cohere intellectually, but they are certainly at one from the point of view of expression and emotional impact. *Pilate and Others* is not, therefore, a work likely to leave much of a mark on faith, the Church or Christian philosophy; but it is one which counts very tellingly in the contemporary cinema and artistic biography of Andrzej Wajda.

Jeshua hopes to win over Judas (Jerzy Zelnik, right) at an evening meal

18. Men and Apparitions—*The Wedding*

BY NOW the cinema of Andrzej Wajda is a crystallised concept with recognisable outlines. Its most compelling feature is its pre-occupation with the nature of "Polishness," its struggle to portray and size up his compatriots in the round. A whole string of films, from *A Generation* and *Ashes and Diamonds* to *Ashes* and *Landscape after the Battle* wrestled with this subject, which however historical it might appear to be, proved in Poland to be a carrier of the most impassioned social, political and ideological controversy. I have indicated that in choosing this path, together with its attendant symbolism, together with its myriad quandaries and pitfalls, Wajda was following his country's richest literary and intellectual legacy: Nineteenth-century Romanticism and its revivals at the end of the last and in the current century. Wajda is an avowed and tenacious devotee of this intellectual and aesthetic tradition.

One of the works most strongly anchored in it is Stanisław Wyspiański's "The Wedding" ("Wesele"). Echoes of this play had already appeared in a number of Wajda's films—and also in the fiction of Jerzy Andrzejewski, no doubt its clinching attraction (witness *Ashes and Diamonds*). An acknowledged masterpiece in Poland, "The Wedding" seems to have been regarded by Wajda as something in the nature of an archetype of his art, of his way of seeing the world and humanity, and also of his symbolism. This was the challenge he decided to confront at the beginning of 1972.

Stanisław Wyspiański (1869–1907), poet, painter, stained-glass window designer, was a man with the undoubted stamp of genius. His verse play "The Wedding" opened in Kraków on March 16, 1901, and that same night a legend was born which is still current. The audience in that theatre in Kraków, then a provincial town in what was known as Galicia and which formed part of the Austro-Hungarian empire, were aware that something momentous had taken place. Pilgrimages flocked to the theatre, critics were in raptures, and at one performance the author was even presented by a group of children with a wreath bearing the inscription "44"—a cabbalistic figure used, in a famous prophecy by the great Romantic poet, Adam Mickiewicz, as a cryptogram for the name of the future saviour of Poland! So

Opposite: Daniel Olbrychski as Lucjan Rydel

from the start the seal was set: "The Wedding" was not simply a play, but an apocalyptic, seminal work in Polish culture.

Its point of departure was a social event that had taken place in the Kraków arts world. A friend of Wyspiański, the poet Lucjan Rydel, had married a country girl, sealing the unity of the intelligentsia and peasantry. The wedding party was held in the cottage of the painter Włodzimierz Tetmajer, who was also married to a peasant girl and had settled in the village of Bronowice outside Kraków. The play is ostensibly a poetic account of this wedding which was a conglomeration of "people of all estates"—or more strictly speaking, the Kraków intelligentsia and the local peasantry. It is set in the room next to the celebrations, into which there keeps bursting flushed couples, people carrying on arguments, solitary guests in search of respite. There slowly builds up a drama which has two streams: on the one hand, real figures racily characterised—Host, Journalist, Poet, the peasant Czepiec—whom Wyspiański simply calls "personages," and on the other, the *dramatis personae:* apparitions drawn from history, literature and legend who are, as it were, internal projections, the troubled consciences, the guilty feelings of the characters. They are, as the author announces in Act Two:

> Whatever lurks in each man's heart
> whatever's seen in each man's dreams
> be it sin
> be it joy
> be he milksop, be he lord
> at the Wedding dance he will.

Between the "personages" and the *dramatis personae* there are natural threads: the Journalist is visited by Stańczyk, a court jester and a by-word for political wisdom among Galician conservatives; the Poet by the Black Knight, the epitome of the nation's past glories and might; the Host by Wernyhora, a model of the national sense of mission and leadership; the Gaffer by the blood-stained ghost of Szela, the desperate peasant who led the Austrian-fomented massacre of the Polish gentry in 1848 (Szela is a standing reproach to the national ideal of solidarism); and so on. Wernyhora presents the Host (i.e. the educated man fraternising with the peasantry) with a watchword and a golden horn (a symbol of the national mission). He passes it on to Jasiek (i.e. a peasant), who mislays it in the confusion. Nevertheless, in the morning the peasants assemble outside the

Opposite: Andrzej Łapicki as the Poet

cottage with shouldered scythes, ready to move. All they need is a signal, but this fails to come. Frozen in expectation, they join the wedding guests in a somnambulistic, stupefied dance to the rhythm of a monotonous melody played by a straw man.

An invitation to continual re-interpretation and a staple of the Polish repertoire, Wyspiański's play has in the last seventy years spawned a mass of analysis too vast to be cited. The received (and scarcely arguable) view is that it is a drama of the "visionary" type about Poles and "Polishness," pitched in a key both tragic and satirical. "The demented final dance of all the wedding guests," Professor Kazimierz Wyka, the authority on the subject, has written, "is intended as a symbol of a society drugged by inertia and incapable of action, a society whose paramount mission of leadership has been lost. The symbol of this lost mission is the golden horn."[1] However, the same writer argues convincingly that "The Wedding" also has a significance that is purely local (Kraków) and topical (the years 1900–05). It embodied a specific socio-political programme. On this reading it would be not so much a drama of national conscience as a picture of the dilemmas of the Galician intelligentsia, hitherto inclined to venerate "rustic vigour" when confronted by the burgeoning political activity of the peasantry *circa* 1905.

Whatever may have been the ideological expediencies articulated by the play in 1901, whatever the immediate impulses to its creation, "The Wedding" is a work that has retained a remarkable buoyancy in the Polish theatre. Time may have evaporated its original message, but it has not dissipated the spell it casts over audiences. The greatest of Polish drama critics, Tadeusz Boy-Żeleński, wrote that the poet "succeeded in blending every tone: gravity, nobility, *élan,* pungent acerbity, sarcasm, the *frisson* of a mystery being fulfilled." True enough: in the heightened atmosphere of the wedding party at which people encounter themselves and their phantoms—dreams and nightmares—one can certainly feel the atmosphere of some great mystery. Existence? Nation? History? Realistic comedy and visionary symbolism interlock into a single, magnificently functioning stage mechanism which glitters with scintillating effects. Finally there is the magic of the sonorous verse: its pregnancy and crispness, its riveting rhythm, have resulted in many lines from "The Wedding" passing into colloquial speech as proverbs. Here then are the elements of a certain

Opposite: Ewa Ziętek (Jadwiga) and Daniel Olbrychski

Maja Komorowska as Rachela

literary and stage structure dazzling in its beauty, its rigidly logical development and uninhibited freedom of poetic association, which pulsates with a mounting rhythm and ends like a piece of music on a climactic suspension of all its *motifs.* No wonder that a work of this description was so close to Wajda's heart.

He was anxious to remain faithful to the text and spirit of Wyspiański's play. He and his co-screenwriter, Andrzej Kijowski (himself an acute judge of Wyspiański), made several cuts in the dialogue and added a couple of scenes which open out the action: a long opening sequence of the wedding procession moving from Kraków to Bronowice, Jasiek's ride which leads to the losing of the golden horn. For the cast he rounded up many of his favourite actors, led by Daniel Olbrychski (Groom), Andrzej Łapicki (Poet) and Wojciech Pszoniak (Journalist). He suggested to them a style

Daniel Olbrychski as Lucjan

of performance that departs quite markedly from the standard approach to "The Wedding," making them accentuate the commonplace aspect rather than the bewitchment of the occasion, and speak the verse as if it came naturally. Visually he gave the production distinct affinities with the art of the turn of the century, and particularly with the intriguing painting of Wyspiański himself: some of the frames with their soft lighting possess the same disturbing sweetness combined with piercing melancholy. The atmosphere of the party has been thickened and intensified: there is more movement, agitation, confusion, and alcoholic mist; although the stage has been opened out, it is more crowded. The confessions, conversations and apparitions which one after the other make up the meaning of the drama have been merged into the whole whirligig of the wedding revels. As the hours go by, moods change, and the atmosphere becomes steadily more

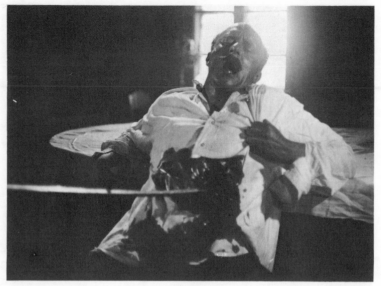

Marek Walczewski in THE WEDDING

charged until there is a feverish expectation of something about to happen, but which fades away in the hypnotic dance at dawn. Some of the conflicts latent in the play have been pointed up: when the peasants collect in response to their mysterious summons and find the Host asleep and dead to the world, they place their scythes to his neck. These scythes are not, therefore, just a part of folk-lore, a nostalgic reminiscence of the gallant scythe-bearers of the Kosciuszko Insurrection a hundred years earlier, but the threat hanging over the Kraków intelligentsia gathered at the wedding in Bronowice.

This is significant. Wajda seems to have mined from Wyspiański's play something that was certainly there but not always visible: the drama of the intelligentsia or, more broadly, of the *élite,* which for all its lumbering

The bloodstained ghost of Szela (Wirgiliusz Gryń)

efforts to integrate with society, remains out of touch, locked up in myths, dreams and arguments which have no counterpart in real life. What comes to the surface in *The Wedding* is not only the drama of this *élite,* but also the drama of the culture of which it was the architect and prime bene- ficiary. For historical and other reasons culture in Poland has been a more fundamental factor of its existence and identity than in other societies. Yet the paradox is that it is deeply rooted in Nineteenth century themes and controversies, which, although often possessing an amazing relevance to contemporary conflicts and dilemmas, belong nevertheless to their own age. Andrzej Wajda's cinema is a good example of this paradox. One can therefore detect in *The Wedding* something of the drama of his art.

157

Pandemonium at the zoo in LOVE AT TWENTY

Filmographies

(compiled by Derek Elley)

Note: ZRF=Zespóły Realizatorów Filmowych (Film-Makers' Units), PRF =Przedsiębiorstwo Realizacji Filmów (Society for Film-Making), WFF= Wytwórnia Filmów Fabularnych (Feature Film Studio), WFD=Wytwórnia Filmów Dokumentalnych (Documentary Film Studio), PWSTiF= Państwowa Wyższa Szkoła Teatri i Filmu (State High School for Theatre and Film), WKF=Wytwórnia Kopii Filmowych (Film Print Laboratory)

A. Feature and short film work

1950: KIEDY TY ŚPISZ (*While You Sleep*) (Poland). Produced by PWSTiF, Łódź. *Dir: Andrzej Wajda. Scr: Andrzej Wajda,* based on the poems by Tadeusz Kubiak. *Ph:* Jerzy Lipman. Short film exercise.

1950: ZŁY CHŁOPIEC (*The Bad Boy*) (Poland). Produced by PWSTiF, Łódź. *Dir: Andrzej Wajda. Scr: Andrzej Wajda,* based on a short story by Anton Chekhov. *Ph:* Zdzisław Parylak. Short film exercise.
CAST: Jan Łomnicki.

1951: CERAMIKA IŁŻECKA (*The Pottery of Iłża*) (Poland). Produced by PWSTiF, Łódź. *Dir: Andrzej Wajda. Scr: Andrzej Wajda. Ph:* Jerzy Lipman. Short film exercise.

1955: POKOLENIE (*A Generation/Light in the Darkness*) (Poland). Produced at WFF No. 2, Wrocław (Ignacy Taub). *Dir: Andrzej Wajda. Ass. dirs:* Konrad Nałęcki, Kazimierz Kutz. *Scr:* Bohdan Czeszko, based on his own novel. *Ph:* Jerzy Lipman. *Cam. op:* Stefan Matyjaszkiewicz. *Art dir:* Roman Mann. *Sound:* Józef Koprowicz. *Music:* Andrzej Markowski. *Played by:* Warsaw Philharmonic Orchestra. *Music dir:* Andrzej Markowski. *Edit:* Czesław Raniszewski. *Cost:* Jerzy Szeski. *Make-Up:* Zdzisław Papierz. 90 mins.
CAST: Tadeusz Łomnicki (*Stach*), Urszula Modrzyńska (*Dorota*), Tadeusz Janczar (*Jasio Krone—"Jaś"*), Janusz Paluszkiewicz (*Sekuła*), Roman Polański (*Mundek*), Ryszard Kotas (*Jacek*), Zbigniew Cybulski (*Kostek*), Ludwik Benoit (*Grzesio*), Jerzy Krasowski, Zofia Czerwińska, Stanisław Milski.
Polish première: Jan. 25, 1955.

KANAŁ: the irony of a scrawled "I love Jacek"

1955: IDĘ KU SŁOŃCU (*I Walk to the Sun*) (Poland). Produced by WFD, Warsaw (Z. Rybarski). *Dir: Andrzej Wajda. Ass. dir:* D. Halladin. *Scr: Andrzej Wajda. Commentary:* Bohdan Czeszko, Ksawery Dunikowski. *Read by:* Aleksander Bardini. *Ph:* Stefan Matyjaszkiewicz. *Ass. cam:* J. Sawicki. *Sound:* Z. Wolski. *Music:* Andrzej Markowski. *Edit:* M. Orłowska, H. Białkowska. 14 mins.

1957: KANAŁ (*Kanal/They Loved Life*) (Poland). Produced by ZRF "Kadr" (Stanisław Adler) at WFF No. 1, Łódź. *Dir: Andrzej Wajda. Ass. dir:* Kazimierz Kutz, Janusz Morgenstern, Maria Starzeńska, Anna Janeczkowa. *Scr:* Jerzy Stefan Stawiński, from his own short story. *Ph:* Jerzy Lipman. *Cam. op:* Jerzy Wójcik. *Art dir:* Roman Mann. *Ass. art dirs:* Halina Krzyżanowska, Roman Wołyniec. *Sound:* Józef Bartczak. *Music:* Jan Krenz. *Edit:* Halina Nawrocka. *Ass. edit:* Aurelia Rut. *Cost:* Jerzy Szeski. 97 mins.

CAST: Wieńczysław Gliński (*Lieutenant Zadra*), Teresa Iżewska (*Stok-rotka—"Daisy"*), Tadeusz Janczar (*Corporal Korab*), Emil Karewicz (*Mą-dry*), Władysław Sheybal (*Composer*), Stanisław Mikulski (*Smukły*), Te-resa Berezowska (*Halinka*), Tadeusz Gwiazdowski (*Sergeant Kula*), Adam Pawlikowski (*German Officer*), Zofia Lindorf, and students of the Łódź Film School.
Polish première: April 20, 1957.

1958: POPIOŁ I DIAMENT (*Ashes and Diamonds*) (Poland). Produced by ZRF "Kadr" (Stanisław Adler) at WFF No. 1, Łódź, and WFF No. 2, Wrocław. *Dir: Andrzej Wajda. Ass. dirs:* Janusz Morgenstern, Andrzej Wróbel, Anita Janeczkowa, Jan Włodarczyk. *Scr:* Jerzy Andrzejewski, *An-drzej Wajda,* based on the novel by Andrzejewski. *Ph:* Jerzy Wójcik. *Ass. ph:* Krzysztof Winiewicz, Wiesław Zdort, Zygmunt Krusznicki, Jerzy Szu-rowski, Bogdan Mysliński. *Art dir:* Roman Mann. *Ass. art dirs:* Leszek Wajda, Jarosław Switoniak, Marian Kowaliński. *Sound:* Bogdan Bień-kowski. *Music:* Jan Krenz, Ogiński ("Polonaise"). *Played by:* Wrocław Radio Rhythm Quintet. *Music dir:* Filip Nowak. *Edit:* Halina Nawrocka. *Cost:* Katarzyna Chodorowicz. *Make-Up:* Halina Sieńska, Halina Turant, Halina Zając. 106 mins.
CAST: Zbigniew Cybulski (*Maciek Chełmicki*), Ewa Krzyżewska (*Krys-tyna*), Adam Pawlikowski (*Andrzej*), Wacław Zastrzeżyński (*Szczuka*), Bogumił Kobiela (*Drewnowski*), Jan Ciecierski (*Porter*), Stanisław Milski (*Pieniążek*), Artur Młodnicki (*Kotowicz*), Halina Kwiatkowska (*Mrs. Staniewicz*), Ignacy Machowski (*Waga*), Zbigniew Skowroński (*Słomka*), Barbara Krafft[owna] (*Stefka*), Aleksander Sewruk (*Swiecki*), Józef Pier-acki, Mieczysław Łoza, Tadeusz Kalinowski, Zofia Czerwińska, I. Orzewska, H. Siekierko, G. Staniszewska, J. Adamczyk, E. Matysik, A. Chronicki, W. Grotowicz.
Polish première: Oct. 3, 1958.

1959: LOTNA (Poland). Produced by ZRF "Kadr" (Stanisław Adler) at WFF No. 2, Wrocław. *Dir: Andrzej Wajda. Ass. dirs:* Janusz Morgen-stern, Sylwester Checiński. *Scr:* Wojciech Żukrowski, *Andrzej Wajda,* based on the novel by Wojciech Żukrowski. *Ph:* Jerzy Lipman (Agfacolor). *Art dir:* Roman Wołyniec. *Sound:* Leszek Wronko. *Music:* Tadeusz Baird. *Played by:* Warsaw National Philharmonic Orchestra. *Music dir:* W. Ro-wicki. *Edit:* Janina Niedżwiecka, Lena Deptuła. *Cost:* Lidia Gryś, Jan Ba-nucha. *Make-Up:* Stefan Szczepański, Roman Baszkiewicz. *Military adviser:* Karol Rommel. 89 mins.
CAST: Jerzy Pichelski (*Captain Chodakiewicz*), Adam Pawlikowski (*Lieu-tenant Wodnicki*), Jerzy Moes (*Ensign Grabowski*), Mieczysław Łoza

(*Sergeant-Major Latoń*), Bożena Kurowska (*Ewa*), Roman Polański, B. Dardziński, H. Dzieszyński, Wiesław Gołas, T. Kosudarski, H. Hunko, A. Młodnicki, I. Małkiewicz, T. Somogi, W. Wozniak, M. Wiśniewski.
Polish première: Sept. 27, 1959.

1960: NIEWINNI CZARODZIEJE (*Innocent Sorcerers*) (Poland). Produced by ZRF "Kadr" (Stanisław Adler) at WFF No. 1, Łódź. *Dir: Andrzej Wajda. Ass. dirs:* Paweł Komorowski, J. Karwowski, U. Orczykowska. *Scr:* Jerzy Andrzejewski, Jerzy Skolimowski. *Ph:* Krzysztof Winiewicz. *Art dir:* Leszek Wajda. *Sound:* Leszek Wronko, L. Księżak. *Music:* Krzysztof T. Komeda. *Song:* Sława Przybylska. *Edit:* W. Otocka, Aurelia Rut. 86 mins. CAST: Tadeusz Łomnicki (*Bazyli/Andrzej*), Krystyna Stypułkowska (*Pelagia/Magda*), Wanda Koczewska (*Mirka*), Zbigniew Cybulski (*Edmund*), Roman Polański (*Polo*), Krzysztof T. Komeda (*Komeda*), Halina Jędrusik-Dygatowa (*Journalist*), Teresa Szmigielówna (*Nurse*), Jerzy Skolimowski (*Boxer*), Andrzej Nowakowski.
Polish première: Dec. 17, 1960.

Wajda and crew on SIBERIAN LADY MACBETH

Olivera Marković in SIBERIAN LADY MACBETH

1961: SAMSON (Poland). Produced by ZRF "Kadr" and "Droga" (Stanisław Daniel) at WFF No. 1, Łódź. *Dir: Andrzej Wajda. Ass. dir:* Andrzej Żuławski. *Scr:* Kazimierz Brandys, *Andrzej Wajda,* based on the novel by Kazimierz Brandys. *Ph:* Jerzy Wójcik (Dyaliscope). *Art dir:* Leszek Wajda. *Music:* Tadeusz Baird. 117 mins.
CAST: Serge Merlin *(Jakub Gold—"Samson"),* Alina Janowska *(Lucyna),* Jan Ciecierski *(Malina),* Elżbieta Kępińska *(Kazia),* Tadeusz Bartosik *(Pankrat),* Władysław Kowalski *(Young Prisoner),* Beata Tyszkiewicz *(Stasia),* Irena Netto *(Mother),* Jan Ibbel *(Genio),* Roman Polański. *Polish première:* Sept. 11, 1961.

1962: SIBIRSKA LEDI MAGBET *(Siberian Lady Macbeth/Lady Macbeth of Mtsensk/Fury Is a Woman)* (Yugoslavia). Title in Poland: *Sybirska Lady Makbet.* Produced by Avala Film, Belgrade. *Dir: Andrzej Wajda. Scr:* Sveta Lukić, based on the novel "Ledi Magbet mtsenskovo uyezda/ Lady Macbeth of Mtsensk District" by Nikolay Leskov. *Ph:* Aleksandar

Sekulović (CinemaScope). *Art dir:* Miomir Denić. *Music:* Dmitri Shosta-kovich. *Cost:* Mira Glisić. 94 mins.
CAST: Olivera Marković (*Katerina Izmaylova*), Ljuba Tadić (*Sergey*), Miodrag Lazarević (*Zinovi Borisovich Izmaylov*), Bojan Stupica (*Boris Izmaylov*), Kapitalina Erić, Branka Petrić, Ingrid Lotarijus, Spela Rozin.

1962: L'AMOUR À VINGT ANS (*Love at Twenty*) (France/Italy/Japan/Poland). Polish episode: *Warszawa* (*Warsaw*). Produced by ZRF "Kamera," Warsaw. *Dir: Andrzej Wajda. Ass. dir:* Andrzej Żuławski. *Scr:* Jerzy Stefan Stawiński. *Ph:* Jerzy Lipman (CinemaScope). *Music:* Jerzy Matyaszkiewicz. 123 mins. (combined running time).
CAST: Barbara [Kwiatkowska-]Lass (*Basia*), Zbigniew Cybulski (*Zbyszek*), Władysław Kowalski (*Władek*).
French première: Jun. 22, 1962.

1965: POPIOŁY (*Ashes*) (Poland). Produced by ZRF "Rytm" (Włodzimierz Śliwiński, Konstanty Lewkowicz). *Dir: Andrzej Wajda. Ass. dirs:* Andrzej Żuławski, Andrzej Brzozowski. *Scr:* Aleksander Ścibor-Rylski, based on the novel by Stefan Żeromski. *Ph:* Jerzy Lipman (Franscope). *Art dir:* Anatol Radzinowicz. *Music:* Andrzej Markowski. *Cost:* Ewa Starowieyska, Jerzy Szeski. 233 mins. (shortened version: c. 110 mins.).
CAST: Daniel Olbrychski (*Rafał Olbromski*), Pola Raksa (*Helena de With*), Bogusław Kierc (*Krzysztof Cedro*), Beata Tyszkiewicz (*Princess Elżbieta Gintult*), Piotr Wysocki (*Prince Gintult*), Józef Duriasz (*Piotr, Rafał's Brother*), Władysław Hańcza (*Rafał's Father*), Jadwiga Andrzejewska (*Rafał's Mother*), Stanisław Zaczyk (*Prince Józef Poniatowski*), Jan Świderski (*General Sokolnicki*), Jan Nowicki (*Captain Wyganowski*), Jan Koecher (*de With*), Janusz Zakrzeński (*Napoléon*), plus 130 other actors and 1,000 extras.
Polish première: Sept. 25, 1965.

1967: GATES TO PARADISE (Great Britain). Produced by Sam Waynberg/Jointex Films Ltd., in association with Avala Film, Belgrade. *Dir: Andrzej Wajda. Ass. dir:* Władysław Sheybal. *Scr:* Jerzy Andrzejewski, *Andrzej Wajda,* based on the novel "Bramy raju/Gates to Paradise" by Jerzy Andrzejewski. *English dial:* Donald Howard. *Ph:* Mieczysław Jahoda (Technicolor, Techniscope). *Music:* Ward Swingle. *Music dir:* Ward Swingle. *Cost:* Ewa Starowieyska. 89 mins.
CAST: Lionel Stander (*Monk*), Ferdy Mayne (*Count Ludovic/Narrator*), Jenny Agutter (*Maud*), Mathieu Carrière (*Alexis*), John Fordyce (*Jacob*), Pauline Challoner (*Blanche*), Denis Gilmore (*Robert*).
Not released (to date) in G.B.

1968: WSZYSTKO NA SPRZEDAŻ (*Everything for Sale*) (Poland). Produced by ZRF "Kamera" (Barbara Pec-Ślesicka). *Prod:* Jerzy Bossak, Ernest Bryll, Józef Krakowski. *Dir: Andrzej Wajda. Scr: Andrzej Wajda. Ph:* Witold Sobociński (Eastmancolor, CinemaScope). *Art dir:* Wiesław Śniadecki. *Sound:* Wiesława Dembińska. *Music:* Andrzej Korzyński. *Music dir:* Andrzej Korzyński, with the participation of the "Troubadours" ensemble. *Edit:* Halina Prugar. 105 mins.
CAST: Andrzej Łapicki (*Andrzej, the Director*), Beata Tyszkiewicz (*Beata, his Wife*), Elżbieta Czyżewska (*Elżbieta, the Actor's Wife*), Daniel Olbrychski (*Daniel*), Witold Holtz (*Assistant Director*), Małgorzata Potocka (*"Flapper"*), Bogumił Kobiela, Elżbieta Kępińska, Irena Laskowska, Tadeusz Kalinowski, Wiesław Dymny, Wojciech Solarz, Józef Fuks, Witold Dederko, Andrzej Kostenko, Wanda Warska (*Guest at Party*), Franciszek Starowieyski (*Guest at Party*).
Polish première: Jan. 28, 1968.

1968: PRZEKŁADANIEC (*Roly-Poly*) (Poland). Produced by ZRF "Kamera" (Barbara Pec-Ślesicka) for Telewizja Polska (Polish TV). *Dir:*

Alina Janowska in SAMSON

Beata Tyszkiewicz and Daniel Olbrychski in EVERYTHING FOR SALE

Andrzej Wajda. Scr: Stanisław Lem, based on his own story. *Ph:* Wiesław Zdort. *Art dir:* Teresa Barska. *Music:* Andrzej Markowski. *Edit:* Halina Prugar. 36 mins.
CAST: Bogumił Kobiela (*Richard Fox*), Ryszard Filipski (*Lawyer*), Anna Prucnal (*Fox's Wife*), Jerzy Zelnik (*Dr. Burton*), Piotr Wysocki (*Dr. Benglow*), Tadeusz Pluciński (*Falsetto Priest*), Wojciech Rajewski (*Man with Dog*), Marek Kobiela.
Polish TV première: Aug. 17, 1968.

1969: POLOWANIE NA MUCHY (*Hunting Flies*) (Poland). Produced by PRF "Zespoły Filmowe" (Film Units) (Barbara Pec-Ślesicka). *Dir: Andrzej Wajda. Ass. dir:* Daniel Olbrychski. *Scr:* Janusz Głowacki. *Ph:* Zygmunt Samosiuk (Eastmancolor). *Art dir:* Teresa Barska. *Interiors:* Maciej Putowski. *Prod. des:* Stanisław Wohl. *Music:* Andrzej Korzyński. *Played by:*

Polish Radio Orchestra, with the "Troubadours" ensemble and A. Nebeski's group. *Music dir:* Andrzej Korzyński. *Edit:* Halina Prugar. 108 mins.
CAST: Małgorzata Braunek (*Irena*), Zygmunt Malanowicz (*Włodek*), Ewa Skarżanka (*Hanka, Włodek's Wife*), Hanna Skarżanka (*Włodek's Mother-in-Law*), Józef Pieracki (*Włodek's Father-in-Law*), Daniel Olbrychski (*Discarded Lover*), Irena Laskowska (*Lady Editor*), Marek Grechuta, Irena Dziedzic, Leszek Drogosz, Jacek Fedorowicz, Artur Litwiński, J. Bratny, L. Bukowiecki, K. Durnatowicz, Witold Dederko, Stefan Friedmann, A. Girycz, J. Kaczmarek, J. Karaszkiewicz, A. Krasicki, T. Lengren, J. Lothe, W. Lothe-Stanisławska, M. Majchrowski, E. Odrobiński, L. Pak, Marek Perepeczko, R. Pietruski, R. Pracz, Jerzy Próchnicki, M. Siatecki, K. Utrata, M. Waśkowski, M. Ziółkowski.
Polish première: Aug. 19, 1969.

1970: KRAJOBRAZ PO BITWIE (*Landscape after the Battle*) (Poland). Produced by PRF "Zespoły Filmowe" (Film Units), Zespół (Unit) "Wektor" (Barbara Pec-Ślesicka). *Dir: Andrzej Wajda. Ass. dir:* Andrzej Brzozowski. *Scr: Andrzej Wajda,* Andrzej Brzozowski, based on the stories by Tadeusz Borowski. *Ph:* Zygmunt Samosiuk (Eastmancolor). *Art dir:* Jerzy Szeski. *Music:* Zygmunt Konieczny, Antonio Vivaldi ("The Four Seasons"), Frédéric Chopin ("Polonaise in A flat"). *Played by:* RTP Orchestra. *Song:* "Gypsy Ballad." *Sung by:* Robert Michaj. 109 mins.
CAST: Daniel Olbrychski (*Tadeusz—"105"*), Stanisława Celińska (*Nina*), Tadeusz Janczar (*Karol*), Mieczysław Stoor (*Ensign*), Zygmunt Malanowicz (*Priest*), Leszek Drogosz (*Tolek*), Aleksander Bardini (*Professor*), Stefan Friedmann (*Gypsy*), Jerzy Zelnik (*Camp Commandant*), Małgorzata Braunek, Agnieszka Fitkau, Alina Szpak, Bohdan Tomaszewski, Józef Pieracki.
Polish première: Sept. 8, 1970.

1970: BRZEZINA (*The Birch-Wood*) (Poland). Produced by PRF "Zespoły Filmowe" (Film Units), Zespół (Unit) "Tor" (Barbara Pec-Ślesicka) for Telewizja Polska (Polish TV). *Prod:* Antoni Bohdziewicz. *Dir: Andrzej Wajda. Ass. dirs:* Andrzej Kotkowski, Krystyna Grochowicz. *Scr:* Jarosław Iwaszkiewicz, based on his own story. *Ph:* Zygmunt Samosiuk (Eastmancolor). *Art dir:* Maciej Putowski. *Sound:* Wiesława Dembińska. *Music:* Andrzej Korzyński. *Music dir:* Jan Pruszak. *Piano:* Janusz Sent. *Songs sung by:* Łucja Prus. *Edit:* Halina Prugar. *Cost:* Renata Własow. 99 mins.
CAST: Daniel Olbrychski (*Bolesław*), Emilia Krakowska (*Malina*), Olgierd Łukaszewicz (*Stanisław*), Marek Perepeczko (*Michał*), Jan Domański (*Janek*), Danuta Wodyńska (*Katarzyna*), Elżbieta Żołek (*Ola*), Mieczysław Stoor, Jerzy Obłamski, Andrzej Kotkowski, Alina Szpakówna, Jerzy Próchnicki, Irena Skwierczyńska.
Polish première: Nov. 10, 1970.

1972: PILATUS UND ANDERE (*Pilate and Others*) (West Germany). Produced by Zweites deutsches Fernsehen. *Dir: Andrzej Wajda. Scr: Andrzej Wajda,* based on the novel "Master i Margarita/The Master and Margarita" by Mikhail Bulgakov. *Ph:* Igor Luther. *Art dir: Andrzej Wajda. Edit:* Joanna Rojewska. *Cost:* Andrzej Wajda. c. 100 mins.
CAST: Wojciech Pszoniak (*Jeshua*), Jan Kreczmar (*Pilate*), Daniel Olbrychski (*Matthew*), Marek Perepeczko (*Marcus*), Andrzej Łapicki (*Afranius*), Vladek Sheybal (*Caiaphas*), Jerzy Zelnik (*Judas*), and others.
West German TV première: Mar. 29, 1972.

1972: WESELE (*The Wedding*) (Poland). Produced by PRF "Zespoły Filmowe" (Film Units), Zespół (Unit) "X" (Barbara Pec-Ślesicka). *Dir: Andrzej Wajda. Scr:* Andrzej Kijowski, based on the play by Stanisław Wyspiański. *Ph:* Witold Sobociński (Eastmancolor). *Art dir:* Tadeusz Wybult. *Music:* Stanisław Radwan. *Edit:* Halina Prugar. *Cost:* Krystyna Zachwatowicz. 106 mins.
CAST: Daniel Olbrychski (*Lucjan Rydel*), Ewa Ziętek (*Jadwiga Mikołajczyk*), Małgorzata Lorentowicz (*Radczyna*), Barbara Wrzesińska (*Maryna*), Andrzej Łapicki (*Poet*), Wojciech Pszoniak (*Journalist/Stańczyk*), Marek Perepeczko (*Jasiek*), Maja Komorowska[-Tyszkiewicz] (*Rachela*), Franciszek Pieczka (*Czepiec*), Marek Walczewski (*Host*), Emilia Krakowska (*Marysia*), Gabriela Kwasz (*Zosia*), Maria Konwicka (*Haneczka*), Mieczysław Voit (*Jew*), Henryk Borowski (*Grandfather*), Hanna Skarżanka (*Klimina*), Iza Olszewska (*Hostess*), Andrzej Szczepkowski (*Nos*), Mieczysław Czechowicz (*Priest*), Kazimierz Opaliński (*Father*), Bożena Dykiel (*Kasia*), Mieczysław Stoor (*Wojtek*), Janusz Bukowski (*Kasper*), Leszek Piskorz (*Staszek*), Ania Góralska (*Isia*), Artur Młodnicki (*Wernyhora*), Olgierd Łukaszewicz (*Ghost*), Czesław Wołłejko (*Hetman*), Wirgiliusz Gryń (*Phantom—Szela*), Czesław Niemen (*Chochoł*).
Polish première: Jan. 8, 1973, Kraków.

B. Theatre works

1959: A HATFUL OF RAIN by Michael Vincente Gazzo. Translated into Polish by Kazimierz Piotrowski, under the title "Kapelusz pełen deszczu." *Produced and designed by Andrzej Wajda. Cost:* Zofia Żuchowska.
CAST: Zbigniew Cybulski (*Johnny*), Edmund Fetting (*Pol*), Mirosława Dubrawska (*Celia*).
Première: May 1, 1959, at "Teatr Wybrzeża" in Gdańsk.

Ryszard Filipski and Jerzy Zelnik in ROLY-POLY

1960: HAMLET by William Shakespeare. Translated into Polish by Roman Brandstaetter. *Produced and designed by Andrzej Wajda. Music:* Tadeusz Baird. *Choreog:* Janina Jarzynówna.
CAST: Edmund Fetting (*Hamlet*), Elżbieta Kępińska (*Ophelia*), Stanisław Iżykowski (*Fortinbras*), Tadeusz Gwiazdowski (*Polonius*), Zbigniew Wójcik (*Claudius*), Jerzy Goliński (*Horatio*).
Première: Aug. 13, 1960, at "Teatr Wybrzeża" in Gdańsk.

1960: TWO FOR THE SEESAW by William Gibson. Translated into Polish by Kazimierz Piotrowski and Stanisław Zieliński, under the title "Dwoje na huśtawce." *Produced by Andrzej Wajda. Designer:* Zofia Wajda.
CAST: Elżbieta Kępińska (*Gizella*), Zbigniew Cybulski (*Jerry*).
Première: Dec. 23, 1960, at "Teatr Ateneum, Scena 61" in Warsaw.

1962: WESELE (*The Wedding*) by Stanisław Wyspiański. *Produced and designed by Andrzej Wajda. Music:* Jerzy Kaszycki. *Choreog:* Zofia Więcławówna.
CAST: Izabela Olszewska, Jerzy Nowak, Leszek Herdegen, J. Haniszówna, Artur Młodnicki.
Première: Oct. 26, 1962, at "Teatr Stary" in Kraków.

1963: THE DEVILS by John Whiting. Translated into Polish by Krystyna Tarnowska and Andrzej Nowicki, under the title "Demony." *Produced by Andrzej Wajda. Designer:* Ewa Starowieyska and *Andrzej Wajda. Cost:* Ewa Starowieyska.
CAST: Jerzy Duszyński (*Father Grandier*), Aleksandra Śląska (*Joan*), Krystyna Bryll, Marian Kociniak, Jan Matyjaszkiewicz, Janusz Wilhelmi.
Première: Mar. 15, 1963, "Teatr Ateneum" in Warsaw.

1970: PLAY STRINDBERG by Friedrich Dürrenmatt. Translated into Polish by Zbigniew Krawczykowski. *Produced and designed by Andrzej Wajda. Music:* Jerzy Maksymiuk. *Choreog:* Gerard Wilk.
CAST: Barbara Krafft (*Alicia*), Tadeusz Łomnicki (*Edgar*), Andrzej Łapicki (*Kurt*).
Première: Mar. 19, 1970, "Teatr Współczesny" in Warsaw.

1971: BIESY (*The Possessed*). Based on the adaptation by Albert Camus of the novel "Byesy/The Devils" by Fyodor Dostoyevski. Translated into Polish by Joanna Guze. *Produced and designed by Andrzej Wajda. Cost:* Krystyna Zachwatowicz. *Music:* Zygmunt Konieczny. *Assistants to Wajda:* Kazimierz Kaczor, Marek Rozynek.
CAST: Wojciech Pszoniak (*Pyotr Stepanovich Verkhovenski*), Andrzej Kozak (*Alexey Kirillov*), Jan Nowicki (*Stavrogin*), Zofia Niwińska (*Varvara Petrovna Stavrogin*), Hanna Halcewicz (*Liza Drozdov*), Marta Rippel (*Matriosha*), Marek Walczewski (*Tikhon*), Tadeusz Malak (*Narrator*), Aleksander Fabisiak (*Ivan Shatov*), Izabela Olszewska (*Maria Timofeyevna Lebyatkin*), Jerzy Binczycki (*Captain Lebyatkin*), Celina Niedźwiecka (*Praskovya Ivanovna Drozdov*), Maria Rabczyńska (*Dasha Shatov*), Wiktor Sadecki (*Stepan Trofimovich Verkhovenski*), Janusz Sykutera (*Liputin*), Wojciech Ruszkowski (*Shigalov*), Jerzy Baczek (*Virginski*), Leszek Piskorz (*Student*), Marian Słojkowski (*Lyamshin*), Euzebiusz Luberadzki (*Alexey Yegorovich, the Butler*), Rajmund Jarosz (*Maurice Nikolayevich*), Kazimierz Kaczor (*Fedka*), Wanda Kruszewska (*Virginska*),

Danuta Maksymowicz (*Schoolgirl*), Ferdynand Wójcik (*Captain* and *Priest*), Elżbieta Karkoszka (*Marie Shatov*).
Première: Apr. 29, 1971, "Teatr Stary" in Kraków.

1972: STICKS AND BONES by David Rabe. Translated into Russian by I. Irov, under the title "Kak brat bratu/As Brother to Brother." *Produced and designed by Andrzej Wajda. Music:* A. Lubitski.
CAST: Oleg Tabakov (*Rick*), Lila Tolmacheva (*Harriet*), Valeri Gaft (*Ossie*), Igor Kvasha (*David*), D. Ivanova (*Girl*), A. Vokach (*Father Donald*).
Première: Dec. 26, 1972, "Sovremennik" Theatre in Moscow.

C. TV-Theatre Works

1962: WYWIAD Z BALLMAYEREM (*Interview with Ballmayer*) from the novel of the same title by Kazimierz Brandys. *Produced by Andrzej Wajda. Art dir:* J. Banucha.
CAST: Władysław Krasnowiecki (*Ballmayer*), Gustaw Holoubek (*Daves*), Beata Tyszkiewicz (*Inga*), Janusz Paluszkiewicz (*John*).
TV première: Jun. 11, 1962.

1962: CUDZA ŻONA I MĄŻ POD ŁOŻKIEM (*Another's Wife and Husband under the Bed*), adapted by J. Jaxa from a story by Fyodor Dostoyevski. Translated into Polish by Gabriel Karski. *Produced by Andrzej Wajda. Art dir:* J. Banucha.
CAST: Wojciech Siemion, Ignacy Gogolewski, Alina Janowska, Andrzej Łapicki, Kazimierz Opaliński.
TV première: Nov. 26, 1962.

1969: MACBETH by William Shakespeare. Translated into Polish by Jerzy Sito. *Produced by Andrzej Wajda. Art dir:* Jerzy Szeski. *Music:* Adam Sławiński.
CAST: Tadeusz Łomnicki (*Macbeth*), Magdalena Zawadzka (*Lady Macbeth*), Daniel Olbrychski, Andrzej Łapicki, Ryszard Pietruski, Jan Englert.
TV première: Apr. 30, 1969.

D. Work as scriptwriter

1953: *Trzy opowiesci* (*Three Stories*) (with Antoni Bohdziewicz, Bohdan Czeszko; *dirs:* Konrad Nałęcki, Ewa Petelska, Czesław Petelski).

1956: *Apel poległych* (*Roll of Honour*) (*dir:* Bohdan Poręba).

Footnotes

Introduction
[1] "Cahiers du cinéma," no. 102, 1959.

Chapter One
[1] From an interview with Bolesław Michałek, "Kino," no. 1, 1968.
[2] From an interview with Bolesław Sulik recorded on March 2, 1967, for the British Film Institute in London.
[3] From an interview with Bolesław Michałek, for Belgian television, quoted from Hadelin Trinon, "Andrzej Wajda," Editions Seghers, Paris, 1964, p. 112.
[4] Interview with Bolesław Sulik, *op. cit.*

Chapter Three
[1] Interview with Bolesław Michałek, from Hadelin Trinon, *op. cit.,* p. 112.
[2] *ibid,* p. 111.
[3] *ibid,* p. 112.
[4] *ibid,* p. 112.
[5] *ibid,* p. 180.
[6] "Positif," no. 21, February 1957.
[7] Antoni Bohdziewicz, "Cypresses and Stone-Pines along the Vistula?" ("Czyżby cyprysy i pinie na Powiślu?"), Łódź Literacka, II/III/1955.

Chapter Four
[1] Andrzej Wajda, 'A Director's Notebook,' "Teatr i film," no. 1/11, 1957.
[2] *ibid.*
[3] Krzysztof Teodor Toeplitz, in a discussion 'Talking of Drama: Back to *Kanał,'* "Dialog," August 1957, p. 118.
[4] Kazimierz Dębnicki, 'Against and For,' "Film," 19/1957.
[5] Leon Bukowiecki, "Dziennik polski," April 25, 1957.
[6] 'The Army Enters the Sewers,' "Trybuna ludu," April 24, 1957.

Chapter Five
[1] Bohdan Węsierski, 'Ashes and Diamonds Not Recovered in the Face of Death,' "Express wieczorny," October 3, 1957.
[2] 'The Killer from the Café de Drainpipe Trousers,' "Trybuna literacka," no. 41/49, 1958.

3 Aleksander Jackiewicz, 'When Poland Exploded,' "Trybuna ludu," October 5, 1958.
4 Roman Szydlowski, 'The Tragedy of a Generation,' "Film," 46/1958.
5 'Andrzej Wajda Speaking,' "Kino," no. 1, 1968.

Chapter Six
1 Stanisław Grzelecki, 'The Poetry of Props,' "Zycie Warszawy," October 8, 1959.
2 Hadelin Trinon, *op. cit.*, p. 113.
3 Jerzy Peltz, 'A Romantic Reportage,' "Film," no. 45, 1958.
4 'For *Lotna*, against *Lotna*,' "Film," no. 44, 1959.
5 Zygmunt Kałużyński, "A Ticket to the New Age" ("Bilet wstępu do nowego wieku"), WAiF, Warsaw, 1963, p. 248.

Chapter Seven
1 Andrzej Wajda, 'A Director's Diary,' in his private collection, quoted from Barbara Mruklik, "Andrzej Wajda," *op. cit.*, p. 62.
2 'Andrzej Wajda Speaking,' "Kino," January 1968, p. 43.
3 *Innocent Sorcerers,'* "Trybuna ludu," December 23, 1960.
4 'Sorcerers or Spellbound?', "Zycie Warsawy," December 20, 1960.

Chapter Eight
1 Barthélemy Amengual, 'En proie à l'histoire,' in Etudes Cinématographiques, "Andrzej Wajda," M. J. Minard, Paris, 1968, p. 66.
2 Andrzej Kijowski, 'Anty-Wajda,' "Przeglad kulturalny," no. 38, 1961.
3 Konrad Eberhardt, 'Samson among the Philistines,' "Film," no. 42, 1961.
4 Barbara Mruklik, *op. cit.*, p. 53.

Chapter Nine
1 'Andrzej Wajda Speaking,' "Kino," January 1968.
2 *ibid.*
3 René Prédal, 'Une lecture shakespearienne de Leskov,' in Etudes Cinématographiques, "Andrzej Wajda," no. 69/72, M. J. Minard, Paris, 1968.
4 *ibid*, p. 162.

Chapter Ten
1 Hadelin Trinon, *op. cit.*, p. 121.
2 *ibid.*

3 Aleksander Jackiewicz, 'The Twenty-Year-Olds,' "Zycie literackie," no. 29, 1965.
4 Hadelin Trinon, *op. cit.,* p. 118.

Chapter Eleven
1 Andrzej Żuławski, 'The Hounds Won't Take to the Woods,' "Film," no. 11, 1964.
2 Andrzej Żuławski, 'Off the Ground,' "Film," no. 28/29, 1964.
3 Wiktor Woroszylski, 'Żeromski Alive,' "Film," no. 41, 1965.
4 Andrzej Żuławski, 'Climates,' "Film," no. 26, 1965.
5 Barbara Mruklik, "Andrzej Wajda," WAiF, Warsaw, 1969.
6 Rafał Marszałek, 'Our Classics,' "Współczesność," no. 2, 1965.
7 Kazimierz Wyka, *'Ashes* Viewed and Discussed,' "Polityka," no. 46, 1965.
8 Stefan Żółkiewski, 'Poetry and Social Passion,' "Film," no. 42, 1965.
9 Janina Zdanowicz, 'An Interview with Andrzej Wajda,' "Polityka," no. 38, 1965.
10 Krzysztof Teodor Toeplitz, 'Historical Tragedy and Absurd Tragedy,' "Kultura," no. 40, 1965.
11 Jan Zygmunt Jakubowski, ' "Ashes" Falsified,' "Ekran," no. 42, 1965.
12 Zbigniew Załuski, ' "Ashes" Simplified,' "Ekran," no. 42, 1965.
13 From a television discussion on *Ashes,* reported in "Słowo powszechne," no. 46, 1965.
14 "Stolica," no. 45, 1965.
15 Tomasz Strzembosz, 'A Sad Mistake,' "Stolica," no. 45, 1965.
16 Jan Wyka, "Tygodnik kulturalny," 1965.

Chapter Twelve
1 Quoted from Barbara Mruklik, *op. cit.*
2 Andrzej Wajda on *Gates to Paradise,* private papers.
3 'Andrzej Wajda Speaking,' "Kino," January 1968.
4 Andrzej Wajda on *Gates to Paradise,* private papers.
5 *ibid.*
6 'Andrzej Wajda Speaking,' "Kino," January 1968.

Chapter Thirteen
1 'Andrzej Wajda Speaking,' "Kino," January 1968, pp. 41–42.

Chapter Fourteen
1 From an interview with Andrzej Wajda in "Filmowy serwis prasowy," no. 12/196, 1969.

[2] *ibid.*

[3] Zygmunt Kałużyński, 'A World Poisoned by Women,' "Polityka," no. 35, 1969.

Chapter Fifteen
[1] Maciej Wierzyński, 'Indifference and Impatience,' "Kultura," no. 40, 1970.
[2] Melchior Wańkowicz, 'The Teeth of My Heart,' "Kultura," no. 40, 1970.

Chapter Seventeen
[1] Andrzej Wajda on *A Film for Good Friday,* private papers.

Chapter Eighteen
[1] Kazimierz Wyka, "The Legend and Truth of 'The Wedding'" ("Legenda i prawda 'Wesela'"), PIW, Warsaw, 1950.